THE BEATITUDES

To Evangelize as Jesus Did

Segundo Galilea

Translated from the Spanish
by Robert R. Barr

ORBIS BOOKS
Maryknoll, New York

Second Printing, January 1987

Manuscript editor: Mary J. Heffron

Library of Congress Cataloging in Publication Data

Galilea, Segundo.
  The Beatitudes.

  Translation of: La misión según las bienaventuranzas.
  1. Evangelistic work. 2. Missions. 3. Beatitudes.
I. Title.
BV3790.G2813   1984   266'.001   83-19342
ISBN 0-88344-344-9 (pbk.)

G & M ISBN 7171-1335-3

CONTENTS

1

THE CHALLENGE
OF EVANGELIZATION

The last third of the twentieth century will go down in history as the time when the church sought a deeper sense of its own identity. To this end it undertook its own renewal, redefining its tasks in terms of the primacy of evangelization.

To us in Latin America at any rate this is the face of the church today. For here, despite so many social, cultural, and even ecclesiastical indications to the contrary, the Spirit of God has been leading the church toward a "state of mission." The foundations of the new missionary movement were laid by Vatican Council II; it was formally inaugurated in Medellín (Colombia); and it was confirmed and broadened in Puebla (Mexico), with the inspired contribution of Paul VI in *Evangelii Nuntiandi*.

The church in Latin America faces many challenges, conflicts, and choices as a result. The Puebla document fairly breathes the tension. But this is not the moment to get lost in the woods of academic discussion. Theory is secondary. The post-Vatican II, post-Medellín, post-Puebla church of Latin America has but one central concern: evangelization. Here our church comes face to face with its own deepest identity, with its pastoral and spiritual renewal. Here is the sole operational point of reference, the only starting point for convoking a communion of Christians whose pluralism is legitimate, but whose conflict is sometimes divisive.

The one great challenge to the church and to Christians is

1

evangelization, for this "is in fact the grace and vocation proper to the Church, her deepest identity" (*Evangelii Nuntiandi*, no. 14). To be sure, this challenge implies lesser ones. There is the challenge to convergence and communion of Christians in the task of evangelization itself, which ought not to be carried out in an anarchical or arbitrary way, but ought to be presided over by the successors of the apostles. There is the challenge to be faithful to the truth—to the content of evangelization—as Christ presented it and as the faith of the church proposes it. After all, only the truth will make us free (Jn. 8:32). The liberating evangelization of human beings would have no meaning if it were not communicated integrally.

There is the challenge to evangelize according to criteria that are authentically Christian. The church has the responsibility of setting forth these criteria in each successive stage of history. They are indispensable if evangelization is to maintain its truth and preserve its identity, if it is to be liberating and redeeming, if, in a word, it is to be Christian. For we are not just engaged in some activity or other that we casually dub "evangelization." This is the activity of Jesus himself, as carried on in the church today.

In order that evangelization be truly Christian, as the church has recently reminded us in *Evangelii Nuntiandi* and in Puebla, it must fulfill a number of requirements:

1. It must preach and share Jesus Christ as the God who saves, and lead human beings to his allegiance and following.
2. It must be an evangelization "incarnate." That is, it must bring about a transformation of the human beings actually alive in Latin America today, with their history, cultures, aspirations, and social organization—their whole reality.
3. It must be integrally liberating. It must transform selfish, unjust, and sinful persons, groups, families, and societies into a just community of sisters and brothers, a community that will qualify for incorporation into the kingdom of God.
4. It must be missionary. It must be directed primarily to those persons and groups most in need, most de-Christianized, most acutely marginalized.

5. It must find its inspiration in the discipleship of Jesus the Evangelizer, true source of all missionary spirituality.

We know all this, of course. We manage it very well—in pastoral discourse. We know that here we have our finger on the authenticity and credibility—the Christian being—of evangelization. But we face anguishing challenges. How can we ever implement all this? How can we ever convey the gospel to hardened humans like these—people immersed in a society that idolizes money, might, and pleasure? How can we bring the kingdom of God to these exploitative, unjust societies of ours, these selfish, divided human beings, these shattered families, these miserable, marginalized persons, these alienated minorities? And still more challenging: how can we bring the gospel to vast cultural and ideological sectors that consider religion to be simply unnecessary for human fulfillment, for morality, and for work for justice and peace, that even declare religion to be not merely useless, but actually prejudicial to the creation of a just society and the liberation of the human being?

All of us have been tempted to despair. We all feel the powerlessness with which we face these arduous, complex challenges. The kingdom of God seems ever to elude our grasp. We are like a voice crying in the wilderness. Evil and injustice always seem mightier than justice and right. We wonder how we can ever break through the crust of this antievangelical reality, how we can ever redeem such selfishness and exploitation. We are tempted in many ways. We fall into conformity and bureaucracy, pusillanimity and indifference, despair of the work itself. Or we are tempted to substitute "something just as good"—we shall call it evangelization, but in fact we are only looking for immediate results: social activism or power politics.

The basic challenge of evangelization, then, is the challenge of Christian hope, and it is inseparable from missionary daring and creativity. Here is a hope rooted not in mere utopias but in reality. For reality today betrays the presence of the kingdom. Our hope is not based on illusions, but on promises that Jesus has already begun to keep. Part and parcel of the Christian task is to give an account of the reasons for its hope (cf. 1 Pet. 3:15) and to discover the seeds of that hope's fulfillment in the very texture of modern life. Evangelization has already borne fruit. There are oases of solidarity and justice in the midst of the selfishness and exploitation we see about us. There is a defense of the dignity and worth of the individual amid this sectarianism and abuse of wealth, power, and sex. The faith persists in the midst of persecution, and people dedicate themselves to God in a morass of materialism. Violence grows faint, and a world of peace is created. Materialist ideologies crumble and give way to the building of just societies and a community of brothers and sisters. Human beings are delivered as through a latter-day flood, by a new Noah's ark.

But in order to further this work of redemptive liberation we must see evangelization from the viewpoint of Jesus and his evangelizing practice. Evangelization is the following of Christ the Evangelizer and cooperation with him in his evangelizing praxis or it is nothing. Either mission arises from faith in Jesus, love for him, and hope in his cause, or it is a "mission impossible."

Spirituality and Mission

Evangelization is the following of Christ as Evangelizer and Redeemer of his sisters and brothers, members of this sinful society. Like every aspect of the following of Jesus, evangelization generates its own spirituality. It is a spirituality with a dynamism for mission; it is a missionary spirituality.

Christian evangelization should be animated by a "mystique" in the original sense of the word—a spirituality, which will penetrate us and identify us with Jesus' mission, and which will become our deepest and most radical motivation for that mission. Missionary spirituality is not merely a set of demands and practices more or less parallel to mission and its tasks—a kind of guarantee of fidelity to these demands and practices. Missionary spirituality is mission itself, with its criteria, attitudes, and options, all animated by the spirit of Jesus. Mission and spirituality are cohesive and inseparable, as soul and body are cohesive and inseparable.

This rootedness in the discipleship of Jesus is the only means we have of creating the "dynamism for mission" which evangelization today so desperately needs, and without which, as we have said, evangelization will never be fully Christian. By "missionary dynamism'' we mean the preferential thrust of evangelization toward the most needy, the de-Christianized, and those on the periphery of society. Evangelization should seek to save the one lost sheep, not the ninety-nine faithful (cf. Lk. 15:3-7). It should seek out the sick, the sinners, not the well or the just (cf. Mt. 9:12-13). It should stride out beyond the frontiers of the church. The missionary accent should put us on our guard against an evangelization that burns itself out in the practicing Christian world of the already converted.

It is essential, then, that Christian evangelization be missionary. Hence it must make certain choices. Some of us are not comfortable with the notion that the church should make choices. Is the church not a church for everyone? Are not all human beings in need of salvation? Are not all called to be the daughters and sons of God? Are not all human beings sinners, little or great? And yet evangelization must follow in the footsteps of Christ the Missioner: hence it must make choices. Like Jesus, mission discerns, in a given concrete reality, which situations and human groups are the most afflicted and alienated and extends privileges to them, thereby revealing the mercy of God, which is made manifest in misery. Choices, then, to the extent that they are the choices of Christ, are part and parcel of spirituality, and belong to the Christian criteria of evangelization.

But which choices are essential to evangelization? Which criteria are inseparable from being Christian? What spirit, what attitudes should be those of the evangelizer, in order to identify with the missionary Christ?

To respond to these questions with our life is to evangelize as Jesus did. Apart from Jesus and his missionary practice, we have no reply.

The Christ We Believe in, Follow, and Share with Others

A priori we do not know what evangelization is. We are ignorant of its content, the criteria for its activity, and the demands it will make on the evangelizer. We are completely in the dark—until we enter into Jesus Christ the Evangelizer—into his criteria, orientations, and attitudes, as the gospel reveals them to us and the faith of the church communicates them.

Our faith in and knowledge of Christ is essential and decisive in the work of evangelization, for the central message of evangelization is Christ. But, let us note, the evangelizer transmits his or her own image of Christ, with the criteria, orientations, and demands that this image contains and implies.

Thus we have a problem. The Christ, and the God, whom we convey to others and share with others is our own personal Christ and our own personal God. We Christians often tend to think that the problem of Christ has already been resolved in our Christian life and pastoral praxis. We believe in him. We accept the truths of faith concerning Jesus. He is God's Son, become a human being like ourselves; he is our Savior; he died, rose, and is alive again forever, humanity's only hope. Christ seems assured and acquired. Thus the correct point of departure for evangelization is already established.

The problems and confusion about mission (we like to think) lie elsewhere. They have to do with church institutions, or various and sundry theological, ethical, or disciplinary questions. Evangelization's problems stem from the complexity of its fields of activity, its relationships with other areas of human endeavor. After all, we reason, evangelization is concerned with human development, and hence must come in touch with all the various cultures, with social liberation, with popular piety, and so on. Evangelization may even brush up against questions of politics, ideology, and pedagogy. It raises all sorts of methodological conundrums. Yes, we confess, there are problems. And they are all grist for the mill of confusion. But the message about Christ —we like to think—is clear. In other areas, pluralism is the order of the day. We may even disagree among ourselves as to the manner and orientations of evangelization because of the complexities just mentioned, for all of these complexities imply value judgments, and value judgments vary according to the school of thought. The evangelizing corps is recruited from many Christian sectors. There is bound to be disagreement as to the *manner* of evangelization. But the content? Ah, here at last we have agreement on something. And of course it is the main thing: the Christ we believe in, follow, and endeavor to share with others is common to us all.

But is this really the case? The truth is, we have *not* resolved the problem of Christ in our lives. A priori we cannot be certain that the Christ any of us believes in, follows, and shares with others is fully and authentically the Christ of the church's faith. Often enough we believe in a "distorted" Christ, an incomplete Christ, a Christ adapted to particular interests of our own. And this is the Christ we then convey to others. It is not that we are not really Christian. It is a matter of the need we as Christians have of ongoing evangelization. When it comes to our own Christianity and the idea we have of Christ, we ourselves need to be evangelized. Otherwise we would be complete saints. To evangelize is to purify someone's idea of Christ, his teaching, and his discipleship. This is what is central. Here lies the crux of so many problems and so much confusion about the church and its mission. In large part these problems and this confusion are problems and confusion about Christ himself, his work, and his teaching.

It was not by chance that, in listing the conditions for evangelization in his opening address at Puebla, Pope John Paul II spoke first of the truth about Christ. Belief in the true, undistorted Christ guarantees that the Christ we share with others will be true. Jesus risks being manipulated, conditioned, reduced— and if he is, this will automatically condition evangelization and the notion we have of the mission of the church.

This is all confirmed by experience. There are multiple notions of Jesus Christ in Latin America today, and some of them go well beyond the bounds of legitimate schools of spirituality. They succumb to the distortions of an inadequate evangelization, or to ideological or cultural manipulation. The Christ of an Indian of the Andes is different from the Christ of an upper-class Christian. Christian working people pray to and follow a Christ surprisingly different from the one the Christian industrialists, economists, and legislators pray to and follow. Popular piety needs to purify its image of Jesus. But the Christ of an elite bourgeois Christianity, or of the ruling classes, stands in equal need of purification.

Thus some of Jesus' traits are accepted while others are rejected. We willingly draw some of the conclusions of the incarnation and Jesus' solidarity with us in our humanity, while we mute others. Jesus is God, well and good; but he cannot partake integrally of human nature. Or just the other way about,

Jesus is our brother and our teacher, but not so clearly our redeeming God.

This syncopated Christianity has grave consequences for evangelization. According to the missioner's particular image of Christ, evangelization will have sociopolitical implications or it will not. It will be an evangelization of social liberation or it will not. It will call for a change in one's personal life, or it will not. It will be missionary—enfleshed in human cultures—or it will not. It will take up human hopes and strivings, or it will not.

Thus we must ask ourselves what Christ we believe in and evangelize. But here again we are posing the question of the relationship between mission and spirituality. It is impossible to evangelize as Jesus did if we do not follow the real Jesus.

The evangelizer's challenge, then, is the following of Jesus the Evangelizer and Missioner according to the faith of the church. We are called to make the criteria, options, and attitudes of Jesus in his evangelizing our own. To this purpose, we have no reliable guide other than the faith of the church. And the church constantly sends us back to the gospel.

Our objective in this book, then, will be to take up the gospel, under the guidance of the church, and endeavor to discover the ways of evangelization according to the mind of Christ.

To this end we propose to study the teaching of the Beatitudes. We do so because the Beatitudes contain the fullest and most compendious synthesis of Christian spirituality and mission and because they reveal the true face of Jesus the Evangelizer, the One we wish to follow and to share with others.

The Beatitudes: To Evangelize as Jesus Did

It is said that the Sermon on the Mount is the most representative passage in the gospel—that it contains the gospel's core message. The Beatitudes, in turn, are regarded as a synthesis of this central passage: they not only introduce Jesus' celebrated discourse, but also provide a summary of it. A goodly part of the Sermon on the Mount is an elaboration and an application of what Jesus had just outlined more concisely in the Beatitudes.

The Beatitudes are at one and the same time a promise and a demand. Jesus promises his disciples the values of the kingdom of heaven, along with the happiness the possession of this kingdom entails. Now, as with all Jesus' promises, the promise of the Beatitudes is to be perfectly fulfilled only in the kingdom of the end time. Only there will happiness be pure and without shadow. But again, as with all Jesus' promises, the Beatitudes have the potential of partial realization right here and now, as a genuine anticipation of that definitive kingdom to come.

Each Beatitude is likewise a demand made by Jesus on his disciples. Each is part of Jesus' prescription for sharing in the kingdom of God today, for becoming his follower and attaining genuine happiness. This promise, this discipleship, and this happiness—all of them fruits of the Beatitudes—are inseparable one from another.

The message of the Beatitudes is not casually addressed to any and all who might hear it. It is reserved for the disciples of Jesus. In fact, it is not even addressed to all the disciples of Jesus, but only to certain categories of persons (in Luke) and to persons with certain life attitudes (in Matthew). Sharing the Beatitudes does not mean that these persons are suddenly "saved." It means that God is bestowing his "happiness" on them, that he is offering them his kingdom, that he is devoting himself to them, that he is inviting them to follow the path he is showing them. He promises them happiness both here and hereafter—a different sort of happiness, flowing from discipleship, and not bestowed by the "world."

It would not be enough, however, to consider the Beatitudes only as a path to gospel spirituality. The message of the Beatitudes is not solely, or even primarily, a message about human beings and their perfection. It is first and foremost a message about Christ and his kingdom. The Beatitudes reveal what God is, not just what we should be. They teach us what the kingdom of God is, and not just what we must do in order to enter it.

Thus we may say that the Beatitudes apply first of all to Christ—that Jesus is the sole "Happy One," and that, in Jesus, the Beatitudes are not an abstract recipe for spirituality, but the expression of his experience of the kingdom, and of his interior life. The Beatitudes reveal the true face of Christ—his criteria, his attitudes, and his loves.

Consequently, the Beatitudes are an indispensable guide to

evangelization. For evangelization must be faithful to the truth about Jesus, faithful to the truth about the kingdom, and faithful to the imitation of Christ the Evangelizer. The Beatitudes show us evangelization through the eyes of Jesus.

The gospels have transmitted to us two different versions of the Beatitudes: that of Luke and that of Matthew. Matthew has eight Beatitudes; Luke has only four, but he immediately subjoins four "Woes." These are missing from Matthew's version.

This is not the main difference between the two versions, however. Their basic difference is much deeper. The two evangelists are speaking about two different things. Their Beatitudes correspond to different concerns and intentions. To all appearances, both evangelists are reporting the same discourse in two different styles, and in words that are sometimes the same and sometimes different. But in actual fact the two series of Beatitudes are distinct in their content—with the exception of the last in either series, the Beatitude on persecution.

Still, the two versions are cohesive and complementary. Any study or meditation on the message of the Beatitudes ought to approach Luke and Matthew separately; but their cohesiveness and complementarity will be evident.

The difference in the two lists of Beatitudes could be summarized as follows. Luke tells us *who* is "happy" in the perspective of Christ and his kingdom. He lists certain categories of persons, and declares them objectively "lucky" (or "unlucky," in the four Woes), independently of any consideration of their moral condition. By contrast, Matthew tells us *how to become* "happy." He lists the conditions for following Jesus and sharing in his kingdom. Accordingly, Matthew addresses himself to all categories of persons at once.

Both Luke and Matthew, each from his own point of view, teach us in complementarity the conditions under which evangelization will be authentic, credible, and Christian. They show us the road to take if we wish to evangelize as Jesus did. They teach us the criteria, basic options, and proper attitudes of the evangelizer.

The Beatitudes in Luke (which tell us *who* is "happy" according to the nature and orientation of the kingdom of God) reveal the precise predilections and options of the kingdom. They are the predilections and options of Christ. Accordingly they indicate for us the objective options and orientations of evangelization as an activity of the church in promoting the kingdom according to Jesus.

The Beatitudes in Matthew (*how* to become "happy") place before us the exigencies of the attitudes we should cultivate in order to imitate Jesus as Evangelizer. They reveal the attitudes Jesus had, and hence those his followers should have. They reveal the spirituality of the evangelizer who has the mind of Christ. They are concerned with evangelization as life witness.

Luke helps us grasp the great options and orientations of mission. Matthew teaches us the attitudes we should have as witnesses of the gospel. Both dimensions have their source and model in Jesus, the only Happy One and the only Evangelizer.

2

GOD OF THE FORSAKEN

How happy are you who are poor:
 yours is the Kingdom of God.
Happy you who are'hungry now:
 you shall be satisfied.
Happy you who weep now:
 you shall laugh [Lk. 6:20–21].

Each of the first three Lucan Beatitudes is addressed to the same persons. The "poor," the "hungry," and those "who weep" for their afflictions are all the same category of people. They are the destitute, the needy, the poor, the materially forsaken. The social situation of these persons is objectively and in itself dehumanizing, "marginalizing." Here these persons are represented by Jesus' disciples, to whom he actually proclaimed these Beatitudes historically.

He then came down with them and stopped at a piece of level ground where there was a large gathering of his disciples with a great crowd of people from all parts of Judaea and from Jerusalem and from the coastal region of Tyre and Sidon who had come to hear him and to be cured of their diseases. People tormented by unclean spirits were also cured, and everyone in the crowd was trying to touch him because power came out of him that cured them all [Lk. 6:17–19].

12

It is to these sick, these tormented and afflicted, that Jesus speaks.

The Puebla Conference picked up the thread of Christian tradition when it identified the Lucan "poor," for Latin America at least, with the needy, the marginalized, and the oppressed—especially as we encounter them in "the faces" of young children, of frustrated youth without a future, of the native population, of the Afro-Americans, of peasants, laborers, the underemployed and the unemployed, the aged, the human refuse of the cities (Puebla Conference, *Final Document*, nos. 31–39). In other words, "the poor" in Luke are those who suffer oppression and social marginalization.

In Latin America oppression and social marginalization— Lucan "poverty"—are by and large the product of socioeconomic factors, although it must be said that the chronically ill, many of the elderly, and many who suffer forms of discrimination other than purely social or economic are "poor" in the Lucan sense as well. By contrast, the "poor in spirit," what we have come to call "spiritual poverty," which is also part of Jesus' message, will be the subject of the Beatitudes in Matthew. The Christian message is concerned with both kinds of "poverty." There is a connection between them, but they are not the same thing.

Luke proclaims the "poor"—the oppressed, the forsaken—to be "happy" because "the Kingdom of God is [theirs]." That is, the kingdom of the promise is destined for them in particular. (All the Beatitudes promise the kingdom in different figures and images: "You shall be satisfied," "You shall laugh"—or "shall be comforted" in Matthew—"shall have mercy shown them," "shall see God," and so on [cf. Lk. 6:20–23; Mt. 5:3–10].) But to say this—that "the kingdom is theirs"—means concretely that the gospel, the Christian message, and hence the church, belong to them.

What does this Beatitude in particular mean? Or first, what does it *not* mean? It does *not* mean, "It is not important if you are oppressed and forsaken in this life. You shall have your reward in the life to come." No, the Beatitudes are a promise whose fulfillment begins right here and now, and any postponement and relegation to somewhere in "heaven" voids them of their historical content, deprives them of their significance for *today's* evangelization, for *today's* preaching of the gospel. This message would alienate the poor and could even be insulting to them.

Nor does this first Lucan Beatitude mean that Jesus is "canonizing" poverty—that he is transforming it into something good, a source of special values and graces. No, the poor are not particularly good or necessarily better than anyone else. The kingdom is for the poor not because they are good or because they are better than others (Matthew's "spiritual poverty" will be more along this line), but simply because they are poor and needy.

Then how can we grasp what this Beatitude *is* trying to tell us? How is the kingdom, promised to all, for the poor in particular? Let us use a modern comparison.

We are in a miserable little village of the Andes. The vast majority of its people are very poor. There are no health facilities here, no hospital, no medicines, no doctors or nurses. Neither have these poor the money to travel to the city for treatment if they fall ill. So they suffer a great deal from their illnesses, and they die prematurely. In the same village, as often happens, there is also a group of families in more comfortable circumstances. These latter can afford to journey to the city to be looked after, and can afford to purchase medicines. Unlike their fellow villagers, they do not live in deprivation.

One day a clinic is set up in the village. It is well staffed and well equipped. Now the people can be treated for their diseases right in their village. Furthermore the clinic is free. It offers its services and medicines gratis.

Now comes the day of the formal opening. A priest is asked to bless the new facility. He says—this minister of Christ: "You are happy ones today, you, the poor of this village. For this clinic is yours. It belongs to you."

At first glance it may seem that the priest's assertion is not precisely accurate. Actually the clinic is for everyone, is it not? It is free for everyone—everyone in the village, both the poor and the comfortable. So why does the priest mention only the poor?

For a very good reason. It is the poor who have most reason to rejoice, most reason to be "happy" about the clinic. For the poor, more than for those of the village in more comfortable circumstances, the clinic is the fulfillment of an ancient promise. It is "good news." It is a great source of hope. True, the clinic is not for them alone. It is for rich and poor alike. *But its primary beneficiaries are the poor.*

It is somewhat the same with the kingdom, and the gospel promise of the kingdom. The destitute, the abandoned, the forsaken are its primary beneficiaries. It is "good news" first and foremost for them. It is as if Jesus said, "Happy are you who are poor, who are hungry today, who are afflicted, for the kingdom of God that I now inaugurate, the Good News of the gospel, is destined especially for you, is dedicated especially to you. It is for your benefit that it is being established." Or: "Now that the kingdom is beginning to be proclaimed, is beginning to advance, you can expect to be delivered from your slavery. Your liberation is under way. The kingdom is making common cause with you."

Why does the kingdom constitute a solid hope of liberation for the poor and the oppressed? Why this "preferential option for the poor," to which this Beatitude leads us as special sign of the kingdom and earmark of authentic evangelization?

Not for sociological reasons, "because the poor are numerous." And not for moral reasons, "because the poor are good." But for scriptural reasons. That is, for reasons of faith: because of the very nature of the kingdom of God. For if what the church teaches us, following the teaching of Christ, is true—that the kingdom is to be anticipated here in history, and that this anticipation will lead to love, justice, freedom, peace, and a community of brothers and sisters—then the gospel of the kingdom must already be at work today, changing unjust situations into just ones, oppressive ones into liberating ones, divisive ones into communitarian ones. The kingdom is Good News. Hence its action will be to the benefit of those who suffer injustice and oppression, those who are excluded from a society of sisterly and brotherly love and community. And who are these persons? They are the poor—the needy and the forsaken. Hence Luke calls them "happy"—blessed, fortunate.

This Beatitude is more easily understood if we consider it in the context of all of Jesus' activity and teaching. His option for the poor and his identification with them, such important facets

of his life, are presented by him as the credentials of the
kingdom he is establishing, as the sign of its authenticity. He
thereby also establishes an essential trait of Christian evangelization, of which he himself is model and witness.

Evangelizing the Poor

Here let us take two classic texts, also from Luke. In the synagogue at Nazareth, as we read in Lk. 4:16–22, Jesus seeks to
establish the credentials of the message that he has begun to
proclaim. To this purpose he calls to witness the prophet Isaiah:

> The spirit of the Lord has been given to me,
> for he has anointed me.
> He has sent me to bring the good news to the poor,
> to proclaim liberty to captives
> and to the blind new sight,
> to set the downtrodden free [Lk. 4:18].

Evidently, where liberation is concerned, it is the poor who
are the privileged ones.

It is true that these words have an eschatological sense as well.
Jesus' discourse points to a blindness, an oppression, a captivity
deeper and more interior than the mere sociological categories
corresponding to each concept. He is alluding to the blindness,
the oppression, and the captivity of sin. But this full sense is
significant precisely because of Jesus' liberation of human beings from the human blindnesses, oppressions, and captivities
that afflict them.

This becomes clear when we observe Jesus' attitude in proclaiming the Good News. Christ, in the midst of the people,
always joined his call to faith and conversion with a concern for
the deliverance of the poorest from their human servitudes, as
far as he could possibly further that deliverance, and actually
went in search of opportunities for furthering it: "He went
around the whole of Galilee teaching in their synagogues, proclaiming the Good News of the kingdom and curing all kinds of
diseases and sickness among the people" (Mt. 4:23).

We find the same teaching, even more explicitly, in Luke

7:18-23. The followers of John the Baptist, anxious to learn
whether Jesus is the authentic Messiah or whether they are to
"wait for someone else," are dispatched by John to put their
question to Christ personally. But Christ does not give a direct
yes or no answer. Instead he shows them the meaning of his
actions and preaching. Thus the very authenticity and credibility
of Jesus' gospel is at stake here.

> It was just then that he cured many people of diseases and
> afflictions and of evil spirits, and gave the gift of sight to
> many who were blind. Then he gave the messengers their
> answer, "Go back and tell John what you have seen and
> heard: the blind see again, the lame walk, lepers are cleansed,
> and the deaf hear, the dead are raised to life, the Good News
> is proclaimed to the poor . . ." [Lk. 7:21-22].

What Jesus is saying is that this liberation, this deliverance of an
afflicted people from their servitude, and the proclamation of
the Good News to the poor are the guarantee of the authenticity
of his mission.

If we take this passage in the context of the whole gospel
message—especially in view of the mission of the church
today—it becomes extremely interesting. It shows us that the
evangelization and liberation of the poor should be simultaneous. It identifies for us the true nature of preaching that "delivers." It shows us the true nature of a liberating evangelization.

Of course, bodily cures are liberating in and of themselves.
But Jesus' deliverance of the afflicted goes beyond mere bodily
cures. Jesus promotes the social integration, the demarginaliza-
tion, of the afflicted. His cures of possessed persons, lepers, and
the blind are typical. These are the social categories most
favored by his cures, as all four evangelists attest. These are the
miracles which stand out most, and which are reported in the
greatest number.

For it was the possessed, the blind, and lepers who were for
the most part the pariahs, the "outcasts," of this society. Lepers
and the possessed were considered subhuman, despised and
shunned. The blind according to both Judaic and Eastern tradition were under suspicion of sin: blindness was not only a physi-

cal evil, but also a moral evil. "Rabbi, who sinned, this man or his parents, for him to have been born blind?" Jesus' disciples asked him when he was on the point of curing the person who had been born blind (Jn. 9:2). In restoring all these persons to health, Jesus liberated them from a bodily misery and a social slavery at the same time.

Partial, precarious deliverance! Jesus' cures were inadequate. As physical cures they were inadequate, for their beneficiaries were not only still subject to forms of servitude other than disease, but were also capable of falling victim to other diseases as well. The cures were inadequate from the point of view of total liberation, because total liberation goes to the root cause of the oppression of the poor in the prevailing social structures. It was not the mission of Christ to dissolve all the afflictions and solve the whole problematic social structure of his time all by himself. Neither was this the primary purpose of his miracles and cures.

The deeper meaning of these precarious, limited acts of human liberation consisted in their demonstration that the Good News announced by Jesus was authentic and credible. In all their insufficiency, they were still enough to maintain people in hope that the God of Promises, the God of Deliverance, was present here, and had not forgotten his people: "God has visited his people" (Lk. 7:16).

At the same time that he cured the poor, Jesus "brought the good news" to them. He evangelized them. He called them to faith and conversion. He summoned them to what we call "interior liberation"—liberation from their sins, their selfishness, and spiritual slavery. This, for Jesus, is what brings the liberation of the poor to its fullness. It guarantees their deliverance from social slaveries by affording them the interior basis and ultimate meaning of all liberation. For, ultimately, they were hungering "not for food that cannot last," but "for food that endures to eternal life" (Jn. 6:27).

In other words, the poor are not merely socially oppressed and needy, they are also sinners in need of conversion, as all human beings are. In delivering the paralytic from his physical misery (Lk. 5:17ff.), Jesus is presenting the doctors of the law with his credentials as Liberator from sin; and thereby he underscores the principal content of his salvific preaching and action.

Consequently, the first Beatitude, addressed to the poor, the hungry, and the afflicted, does not mean that they are already saved. Yes, the kingdom is theirs. They are its preferred citizens. But they have to accept it. They have to enter it. It is Matthew's version of the Beatitudes that will point out the way to the kingdom.

Let us return for a moment to our parable of the clinic built for the destitute and forsaken population of the Andean village. The mere fact of its existence is no guarantee of the health of the poor or anyone else. People must take advantage of the clinic. They must avail themselves of its services, submit to treatment. They must take their medicine. Similarly, the poor must follow Jesus and his teachings in order to possess their kingdom.

In sum: the first Lucan Beatitude is not primarily a message conveying information about the poor, or about what the poor must do in order to become disciples of Jesus, but a message concerning the orientation, the criteria, and the preferences of the kingdom that Jesus is inaugurating. It is a message and a revelation about Jesus himself, the Evangelizer. He reveals to us his criteria and his orientations, which are the same as those of his Father.

This first Beatitude reveals to us that the God of Jesus Christ, and his kindgom, are primarily for the forsaken and the destitute, and that this is the criterion that evangelization must apply in order to be "Christian," in order to be that service to the kingdom that God desires, and as he desires it.

For the Christian community, living this Beatitude will mean being a community of the poor, a church of the poor. God by his own choice is a God of the poor, the oppressed, and the afflicted. The church, in its best traditions and most official teaching, seeks to be a church of these poor, oppressed, and afflicted, as well. What else can its social teaching, its activity with the poor, and its defense of human rights mean? In Latin America at least, the church's orientations are very definitely toward the interests of the weakest and most afflicted.

This is the basis of a liberating evangelization, hence also of the theology of liberation that supports that evangelization. For the raison d'être of the theology of liberation is not to be sought in its sociological critique, nor in its analyses of dependency and underdevelopment, nor in political ideologies, however useful or even necessary all these things may be for the implementation of justice. The raison d'être of the theology of liberation is to be sought in the very nature of the Christian God, as preached by Jesus Christ and conveyed to humankind by his church today.

Like our Master, we the church are summoned to proclaim, in our words and especially in our deeds, that the just cause of the poor, the hungry, and the afflicted is God's cause, and hence that of the church as well.

Any Christian involvement with the poor—be that involvement pastoral, sociopolitical, or cultural—means laboring to make this Beatitude a reality. The gospel in Latin America has failed to create justice for the oppressed, or a human life for those in misery. But this gives us no license to ignore the words of the Gopel of Luke or the constant teaching of the popes and bishops. On the contrary, it challenges us to examine our Christian fidelity to the incarnation of these imperatives in society, according to the capacities and callings of each one of us.

Vast multitudes of Latin Americans are hungry and systematically afflicted. Jesus called them "happy" because, with his coming and the proclamation of the gospel of the kingdom, the hope of their deliverance had dawned. Whether or not this hope will be brought to fulfillment will depend on the mission of the church and its Christians. And this constitutes an ongoing call to us to renew our lives.

●

Happy are you when people hate you, drive you out, abuse you, denounce your name as criminal, on account of the Son of Man. Rejoice when that day comes and dance for joy, for then your reward will be great in heaven. This was the way their ancestors treated the prophets [Lk. 6:22-23].

This fourth and last Lucan Beatitude, as we have already established, is the only one that is identical with a Matthean counterpart. It is Matthew's last Beatitude too, and hence we shall defer our consideration of its implications for evangelization until our treatment of its Matthean formulation.

3

GOD OF UNIVERSAL HOPE

But alas for you who are rich:
  you are having your consolation now.
Alas for you who have your fill now:
  you shall go hungry.
Alas for you who laugh now:
  you shall mourn and weep [Lk. 6:24–25].

Luke complements his Beatitudes with four "Woes," or lamentations. The first three of these are antitheses to the Beatitudes concerning the poor. They refer to the rich, the satiated, and "you who laugh now"—all images of the rich as contrasted with the poor. But the parallel breaks down where Jesus, who has blessed the poor and the destitute, does not curse the rich. The four Woes are essentially the simple registration of a fact: the kingdom and the service of riches are incompatible. The Woes are like the sounding of an alarm, a serious question posed by Jesus to the rich, a question springing from his great desire to convert and liberate them. They are an expression of Jesus' universal love. He offers the hope of the gospel to everyone, for he wishes to save everyone. But his mercy reaches the rich wrapped in questions.

Thus the Woes reveal to us other characteristics of the kingdom, and hence other characteristics of evangelization. The Lucan Beatitudes offer us God's criteria for evangelizing the poor; the Woes reveal to us his criteria and method for evangelizing the rich.

Who, precisely, are the "rich" in question here? They are not necessarily simply those who are not poor. They are not simply those who enjoy a life of cultural and economic sufficiency, who do not suffer habitual material affliction and deprivation, and who share in the things valued by society. These are not the "rich" in the sense under consideration here, for this level of wealth is desirable for all, and the poor should aspire to it.

The "rich" of the four Woes must be understood in the context of the whole gospel teaching on the rich and riches. This teaching may be briefly stated as follows.

1. The "rich" accumulate possessions without necessity. To the person in the parable who pulled down his barns and built bigger ones, Jesus tells us that "God said to him, 'Fool! This very night the demand will be made for your soul; and this hoard of yours, whose will it be then?' So it is when a man stores up treasure for himself in place of making himself rich in the sight of God" (Lk. 12:20-21; cf. Mt. 6:19-23).
2. The "rich" neither share their goods nor place them in the service of others, as we learn from the parable of the rich person and Lazarus (cf. Lk. 16:19-31).
3. The "rich" elevate wealth, power, prestige, and the like into values in themselves, into "idols." ("Where your treasure is, there will your heart be also. . . . You cannot be the slave both of God and of money" [Mt. 6:21, 24].)

The condition of the rich—understanding "rich" in this sense —is incompatible with the kingdom. They must be converted and become disciples, like Zacchaeus, that paradigm of the rich person who experiences conversion. For Jesus the proclamation of hope for the rich implies deliverance from their riches— liberation from their wealth, power, and privileges.

Just as the poor are "happy" or "lucky," where the kingdom is concerned, simply because they are poor (and not because they may also happen to be good), so the rich are condemned to woe just because they are rich, and not because they may also happen to be evil in other ways. If the rich person is an exploiter, a godless person, and a sinner besides being rich, then his or her situation is of course all the worse, and his or her alienation from the kingdom all the more profound.

This is clear from the account of Jesus and the rich young person who intended to follow him (cf. Mt. 19:16-26). We know from the account that this person was not an evil person, a sinner. He kept the essential commandments. He practiced the observances of his religion. "I have kept all these. What more do I need to do?" (vs. 20). But then Jesus asked him to share his possessions: he called the man's wealth into question. And the youth "went away sad, for he was a man of great wealth" (vs. 22). That is, his being wealthy prevented him from growing in discipleship and hearing the call of Jesus to "come, follow me" (vs. 21).

This episode gives Matthew the opportunity of recording Jesus' stern discourse on wealth and the wealthy: "I tell you solemnly, it will be hard for a rich man to enter the kingdom of heaven. Yes, I tell you again, it is easier for a camel to pass through the eye of a needle than for a rich man to enter the kingdom of heaven" (Mt. 19:23-24).

Why this incompatibility between the kingdom and riches which persists unless those who possess riches allow themselves to be called into question by Jesus' liberating love? The reasons could be summarized as follows. The wealthy have a tendency to close in upon themselves. They forget their sisters and brothers, the needy, and the oppressed. They are likely to grow deaf to the cry of the poor, the cry for justice and the call to solidarity. For, in the Christian view, it is not enough "not to hurt anyone." It is not enough not to be consciously unjust and exploitative. In order to enter into the kingdom, one must live a life of sharing, a life of compassion. This is the teaching of the parable of the rich person and Lazarus. It is the teaching of the parable of the Last Judgment (cf. Mt. 25:31-46), the parable suggesting that solidarity with the needy is the path to the kingdom ("Go away from me, with your curse upon you, to the eternal fire prepared for the devil and his angels. For I was hungry and you never gave me food . . . "[Mt. 25:41-46]).

In the account of the conversion of wealthy Zacchaeus we are shown the other side of the coin. Here we have the reverse of the example given above concerning the insensitivity of the rich toward their brothers and sisters. Zacchaeus undertakes to do justice. He will make restitution for what he has taken unjustly. He will share his wealth with those in need. This is the concrete, necessary path to his conversion. It is also the indispensable road for the rich of all times, the one they must take to arrive in the kingdom (cf. Lk. 19:1-10). " 'Look, sir, I am going to give half my property to the poor, and if I have cheated anybody I will pay him back four times the amount.' And Jesus said to him, 'Today salvation has come to this house . . . for the Son of Man has come to seek out and save what was lost' " (vss. 8-10).

Wealth—or power, prestige, and the like—prevents the wealthy from discovering the identity and locus of genuine values, prevents them from discovering true humanness and the real meaning of their lives. It is particularly easy for the wealthy to be materialistic. It is difficult for them to be religious. Wealth, and all that goes along with it, tends to absorb the human heart and set itself up as an idol. Hence, Jesus' radical challenge: "Sell your possessions and give alms. Get yourselves purses that do not wear out, treasure that will not fail you. . . . For where your treasure is, there will your heart be also" (Lk. 12:33-34; cf. Mt. 6:20-21). "You cannot be the slave both of God and of money" (Lk. 16:13).

Evangelizing the Rich

The "Woes" pronounced upon the wealthy—the "rich," those who "have their fill now," those who "laugh now"— point up Jesus' criteria for evangelizing them. Jesus in no wise identified himself with the rich. But neither did he exclude them from the invitation to the kingdom, for this was a hope he was offering to all. Jesus does not condemn or exclude the rich. He apprises them dramatically of the fact that their salvation is in danger unless they become poor of heart, unless they open up to the needy and enter into solidarity with them—in a word, unless they become just and merciful. It is the Beatitudes in Matthew that will show them the road to conversion.

All this calls for an ecclesial and missionary reevaluation. The evangelizing church must not identify with the wealthy and powerful any more than Jesus did. It must be the church of the poor.

But neither may it condemn or exclude the wealthy. Following Jesus' example, it must question them, not in a spirit of aggression, but with the love of a shepherd.

This attitude is our challenge. The temptation is powerful to attempt to take on the ways of the rich, to acquire their culture and categories, to preach to them a "spiritual," that is, a spiritualistic, gospel, a tranquilizing gospel, a gospel whose only exigencies are those of religious practice and private morality, a gospel that fails to touch on the questions of wealth, economics, and justice. There is also the corresponding temptation to eliminate the wealthy, to cut them off, to exclude them from our mission. But both attitudes are only attempts at easy solutions. They are one-dimensional. No, Luke's demand, like every challenge in the gospel and every missionary proclamation of the truth, is difficult, laborious, and often fraught with conflict.

The evangelization of the wealthy in the spirit of the Beatitudes demands not only a questioning, a reexamination of wealth, but also and above all a proclamation of the Christian meaning of money and wealth and the consequences of this teaching for the life of the follower of Jesus. In Latin America, where so many educational institutions of the church (including universities) have often catered to Catholics of the social elite (and continue to do so), this demand is fair matter for pastoral reexamination.

There is a Christian meaning of money. It is a meaning that has been warped by today's "have" societies of production and profit. The meaning of money, in the Christian view, is to be a sign of the goods of this world entrusted by God to human beings to develop and share with one another. Money has been invented by human beings in order to facilitate the exchange and distribution of goods. Of its very nature, then, money ought to be the vehicle whereby what is superfluous to those who have is transferred to those who have not. Money ought to be in the service of justice, facilitating the equal distribution of wealth.

But in actual practice, money becomes the prime source of injustice and inequality. When it acquired a worth of its own, became a value in itself, it became human beings' master instead of their tool. It lost its value as sign of the goods of the earth, whose masters are all human beings without exception. As an absolute value, money necessarily becomes a source of power, human exploitation, and division.

Money and wealth are a sign of the work of human beings, of their toil, their sacrifices, and sometimes their blood. Capitalism has perverted this signification, twisting it around, according the primacy to profit, while placing labor in the service of profit. We no longer understand money as a sign of the hard and noble toil of farm people, miners, and other proletarians, or of the creative, taxing work of intellectuals. We have taken money and dehumanized it.

Money, then, as sign of the goods of the earth and the toil of human beings, ought, in the perspective of Christ, to be a vehicle of reconciliation and community among brothers and sisters, rich and poor. It ought to be a means of restoring the bonds of justice and equality, broken by the exploitation of labor and the cult of profit in a civilization that worships wealth.

For Christ, those who have more of the fruits of an earth that belongs to God, and therefore to everyone, ought to be but "faithful and wise servants," placed by the master "over his household to give them their food at the proper time" (Mt. 24:45). Thus, as no one is absolute lord of the earth, no one is absolute lord of wealth either. One is only its trustee, administering it in the name of God, as all power and authority are wielded in the name of God.

The church has always intended the reconciliation of sisters and brothers. It is called to effect this reconcilation among human beings; it must lead them to share their wealth, and to recognize and reward the toil of those who produce it. This conviction has become the consistent teaching of the church, and its ardent petition in the Eucharist, that spring and source of all reconciliation. Here the body and blood of Christ, given for the reconciliation of all women and men, rich and poor, with God and with one another, are offered under the signs of bread and wine, "which earth has given and human hands have made" (in the words of the Prayer of Offering), and which represent the Christian meaning of wealth.

The evangelization of the wealthy means reconciling them with their oppressed brothers and sisters, reconciling their

wealth with the design of Jesus for that wealth. The evangelization of the wealthy begins with the establishment of justice with
respect to the goods of the earth, money, and human toil. It
means that wealth must be shared in order to be at the service of
everyone, and that labor must recover its dignity and its primacy
over profit.

4

GOD OF TRUE FELICITY

Alas for you when the world speaks well of you! This was the way their ancestors treated the false prophets [Lk. 6:26].

The first three Lucan Beatitudes and the first three Woes are set up in contraposition. Poor and rich, hungry and satiated, weeping and laughing are mutually opposed. One might expect, then, that this antithetical pattern would be continued in the fourth pair. If the fourth Lucan Beatitude is pronounced upon the persecuted, the fourth Woe, we might expect, will be pronounced upon their persecutors. But here the parallel structure breaks down. The fourth Woe is not concerned with persecutors at all. Evangelization has no part with vengeance. The unlucky, the unfortunate of the fourth Woe are those of whom "the world speaks well"—that is, those who place their happiness, their "beatitude," in appearances and in the opinion of others.

This Woe could seem unimportant in comparison with the solemn declarations of the former three. But such is not the case. Here the Lord goes to the very root of the human heart, to the search for happiness and people's usual notion of happiness. Here he touches the central nerve of humanism. Jesus is reiterating here that the kingdom has essentially to do with happiness. The kingdom *is* true happiness, and thus it unmasks the prevailing, but false, criteria of happiness—external criteria based on appearances, honors, and flattery. These are the criteria of "status symbols," the criteria that rest on the fragile and precarious opinion of others.

28

Those who seek their welfare and happiness according to these criteria are "unlucky," "unhappy." Their search is incompatible with the kingdom, incompatible with the happiness that Christ not only promises for the future but also guarantees for the present.

The happiness of the kingdom is different because the God of Jesus and the criteria of earth are not the same. By contrast with the Woe of false happiness, Luke has pronounced the Beatitude corresponding to true happiness: the happy ones, the lucky ones are those who suffer persecution for their commitment to the values of the kingdom (cf. Lk. 6:22-23). Nor is it just a matter of a different path to happiness. It is above all the revelation of a different God, the revelation of a God who transforms those who suffer persecution—who are hated, excluded, insulted, or rejected for Jesus' sake and the sake of his gospel—into happy persons. This happiness does not feed on a showy, worldly prestige or status. On the contrary, it is nourished by the seeming ill fame of being a follower of Jesus. The first disciples came by this conviction only slowly and arduously, but it taught them to transform their suffering into constant joy. " . . . They left the presence of the Sanhedrin glad to have had the honor of suffering humiliation for the sake of the name" (Acts 5:41).

This theme is central to the teaching of Christ. Further, it reveals to us a trait particularly integral to his image, particularly in conformity with his criteria and scale of values. Jesus as Evangelizer departs decidedly from the prevailing criteria of this world and proclaims fortunate and happy those who, in the eyes of the world, are of little worth, those who seem unhappy. Thus "anyone who exalts himself will be humbled, and anyone who humbles himself will be exalted" (Mt. 23:11-12), just as "the last will be first, and the first, last" (Mt. 20:16).

Evangelization: Preaching the Meaning of Life

All this points up two essential elements for Christian evangelization. Evangelization always means proclaiming the quest for happiness and proclaiming the meaning of life.

It is axiomatic to say that human beings are made for happiness. Thus their objective calling coincides with their deepest thrust and desire. Human beings can err as to the means to happiness, but they cannot err in their identification of happiness as the end to be attained. Even in their vices, their selfishness, and their sin, human beings seek what they understand to be happiness. Of course, here they are mistaken in their understanding, and when all is said and done, they fail to find the happiness they seek.

We are too much made for felicity—"programmed" for happiness—for Jesus' message about God and human beings not to coincide with it. God is human beings' happiness, and his demands and promises coincide with our own thirst for happiness and with the path to its slaking.

This is the reason why the theme of felicity, under the images of life, peace, and joy, is central to the gospel. Even the concepts of salvation and deliverance are intimately bound up with it. The Beatitudes themselves are a promise of, and path to, happiness, as we have already shown. As Jesus' call to follow him, to live and act as he lives and acts, the Beatitudes are an exhortation to true happiness, and the Woes are a warning not to follow the ways of apparent, deceptive happiness.

Christian evangelization, in order to be Christian, must make satisfactory and enlightening answers to the great questions eternally posed by human beings on the theme of "happiness" and "my happiness." What is true happiness? How is it to be sought and found? If evangelization is to respond to reality, to human aspirations and culture, then it must take into consideration that the sole reality and only aspiration common to all human realities and cultures is the desire for happiness. When we join the message of Christ with human searchings for felicity, then we are evangelizing. When we unite the hopes of humankind with the promises of God, then we are evangelizing.

Thus evangelization, of its very nature, is God's program for happiness. But—as the Woes remind us—this program contradicts human beings' earthly desires and the ways of false felicity. It teaches us that a human being is more than just a human being, that his or her happiness cannot be dissociated from the call to be a son or daughter of God in the following of Christ. The paradox of evangelization consists in proclaiming to human beings that their true felicity resides without—outside them-

selves, outside their selfishness, riches, or status—and that the
font of joy and sole trustworthy criteria of felicity are in Jesus,
the Happy One, the Jesus of the Beatitudes. Happy are those
who hear the word of God and keep it! (cf. Lk. 11:28)—fully
happy in eternity, but happy too in the here and now, with a
deep and abiding happiness, however enveloped in the demands
of faith: "Happy are those who have not seen and yet believe"
(Jn. 20:29).

To preach the happiness that human beings seek means to
reveal to them the meaning of their life in all its depth. It means
revealing to them why they live and why they die. The response
to these questions gives direction to the notion we have of happiness, and to our manner of seeking it. The questions are inescapable, and avoiding or postponing them is actually a way of an-
swering them.

Evangelization must plumb the depths of the human heart. It
must penetrate to the roots of life. It must sound the depths of
human culture, too (cf. *Evangelii Nuntiandi*, nos. 18–20), with
the values, criteria, vectors of force, and so on that are the prod-
ucts of the particular meaning each culture assigns to existence.
Hence evangelization must ask questions, and give answers, in
the area of the great conundrums of the human condition: life,
death, suffering, success, failure, good and evil, and, of course,
happiness.

Thus it eventuates that the gospel of the Beatitudes is necessary simply in order to live as human beings. The Beatitudes
teach us how to be authentically human—how to live, die, suffer, toil, struggle, and be happy as human beings. The gospel of
the Beatitudes is not humanism; but it is the condition for
authentic humanism. After all, true humanism is always inspired
by a sense of genuine life.

The gospel of the Beatitudes is not a culture, but it lays down
the conditions for any culture that hopes to lead us to a life that
is fully human. This essential imperative of evangelization is
especially urgent today, in social and cultural atmospheres so
frequently permeated by atheism and irreligion (cf. *Evangelii
Nuntiandi*, no. 55). Today the Christian message can no longer
be presented merely as the Christian way to happiness, nor simply as a religious meaning for life. Today the Christian message

must be unequivocally set forth as a global, integral alternative—the only truly human alternative—to the meaning (or meaninglessness) of the irreligious ideologies and culture of a materialistic consumer society of such deceptive felicity.

The Beatitudes as proclamation and the Woes as denunciation are the alternatives proposed by the God of Jesus Christ to inadequate or dehumanizing philosophies of life. This "evangelical alternative" is not intended to be a set of teachings or ethical norms, but a global, integral message concerning the deeper meaning of happiness and existence, a message made incarnate in Christ, the Happy One. It is a message about the God of Jesus, who is merciful love and not severe, arbitrary might; who is human beings' infinite happiness and not the font of their fears; who is the liberator and humanizer of the poor and the rich and not a sectarian God of the latter alone, a God deaf to the cry of the poor and afflicted.

In a word, evangelization according to the Beatitudes is the revelation that happiness, humanization, and the meaning of life itself, in a world plagued with misery, sin, and unhappiness, are a gift of the God who is given to us in Jesus Christ; and that by accepting this gift we shall have happiness and life to the full, in the actual reality of the world as we find it.

This is the kernel of Luke's message.

5

THE GIFT OF POVERTY

How happy are the poor in spirit;
theirs is the kingdom of heaven.
Happy the gentle:
they shall have the earth for their heritage [Mt. 5:3–4].

Matthew's Beatitudes have a viewpoint quite different from
that of Luke. Matthew is less interested in *who* is "happy"—
Luke's viewpoint—than in *how* to be happy. He underscores the
evangelical attitudes of a follower of Jesus. He presents a program for Christian living. Luke has revealed to us certain orientations having to do with the activity of the kingdom among
human beings, and with the criteria of Jesus as Evangelizer, and
therefore also with the orientations and criteria of evangelization by a missionary church.

Matthew complements Luke. He shows us Jesus' universal
prerequisites for entry into his kingdom. He presents Jesus as
our model, as incarnating these prerequisites himself, and therefore also incarnating the attitudes that should animate a church
that follows Jesus as Evangelizer.

The Beatitudes in Luke are the source of the options and
orientations of Christian evangelization. Matthew offers us the
spirituality of the Christian evangelizer.

The first two Matthean Beatitudes—those concerning the
"poor in spirit" (meaning the poor and the humble of heart,
those who have the spirit of a poor person) and the "gentle"—

may be considered in conjunction, since they involve the same exigency, the same requirement. In fact, the terms are synonymous in the Bible: both denote the *anawim*, the "poor of Yahweh." "Gentle," which in our modern languages denotes a character trait, does not have this meaning in the Bible: it merely means "poor in spirit," or "poor of Yahweh." (The latter expression connotes the spiritual attitude of the "little remnant," the "righteous remnant of Israel," who remained faithful to the true messianic expectations of the prophets, their hearts prepared to welcome the Redeemer and Liberator of the people. Their consummate model is Mary.)

Then what does it mean to be "gentle" or "poor in spirit"? Obviously, Matthew is referring to a different sort of "poor person," and a different kind of "poverty," from the "poor" and "poverty" in Luke, although, as we shall see, there is a relationship between them. Lucan poverty is material, dehumanizing poverty. It is an evil, the fruit of injustice and sin. The kingdom of God is presented as contrary to poverty: the kingdom is the liberation of the poor, and this is the orientation by which authentic evangelization seeks to be guided.

Matthean poverty, on the other hand, is interior poverty. It is a value, a virtue. It humanizes and liberates the disciples. It is a condition for entry into the kingdom, a condition for following Jesus. It is a spiritual requirement for the church, for it is a spiritual requirement for anyone who wishes to evangelize.

The "poor in spirit" are those who humbly place all their confidence in God, who commit their lives into his hands, who refuse to rebel against his will in the face of life's vicissitudes and contradictions. They are confidently open to God, his will, his word, and his kingdom. Their primordial wealth is Jesus and the values of his gospel.

Matthew does not specify evangelical poverty here as to exterior style and practice. Rather, he indicates the basic attitude of poverty, the root of the virtue of poverty. He teaches us that any external poverty that does not arise from this radical confidence in God, from this abandonment into his hands, is pharisaical. It is not liberating, and it is not Christian poverty. It remains on a superficial level, precarious and ambiguous. There are lifestyles of poverty that are motivated by political or pastoral strategies, by temperament or culture, even by pride and hypocrisy. These expressions of poverty are not necessarily humanizing at all. The radical attitude to which this Beatitude summons us is the decisive criterion for the evaluation of poverty.

But Jesus likewise teaches us that poverty is also pharisaical and inauthentic when it is reduced to an interior attitude, to a "confidence in God" not expressed in a lifestyle, not expressed in external and material forms of poverty. Matthew's message is a criterion for every Christian virtue and value: interior disposition must go hand in hand with external practice. Each of these two dimensions is verified in function of the other. In Christian ethics, the interior and the external are complementary.

In this fashion the Beatitude concerning the poor in spirit prepares for Jesus' demand of evangelical poverty as a precondition for following him: "None of you can be my disciple unless he gives up all his possessions" (Lk. 14:33). This commandment (not counsel) of Christ, addressed to all Christians (not just to a few "poverty specialists") is an outgrowth of poverty of spirit as absolute confidence in God. The first Matthean Beatitude promises riches: God and the values of the kingdom. Jesus' commandment is a call to renunciation, to be disposed to leave all one possesses—things, persons, situations, plans, employment —everything that might come between us and Christ and prevent us from following him.

Christian poverty, then, consists in a freedom of heart, a detachment from persons and things. Its purpose is growth in love. Poverty liberates. It delivers a person into the hands of love. As a Christian attitude, it is inspired by a confident love, and is a condition of that love. The resulting liberty is at the service of the dynamism of a boundless charity, a mystique or spirituality that disposes a person to devote himself or herself to mission. The renunciations of poverty are possible only because the person who embraces poverty is filled with the values of the kingdom and has placed his or her confidence in God and his promises. Renunciation has meaning only as the product of hope in greater values than the ones renounced, and it liberates and humanizes only because it deepens freedom and love. What makes poverty Christian is not the renunciation, but the motives of the renunciation: confidence in the God of Jesus and in the reality of his kingdom, in whose riches one already participates. Poverty's task of witness is to reveal, through renunciation, that Jesus and his gospel are absolutely reliable reality.

This poverty of spirit necessarily leads to expression in actual material poverty, in concrete forms of detachment, in a poor and austere lifestyle. As we have said, poverty of spirit without actual poverty would be illusory and vacuous. Further, given the living bonds between action and attitude in human beings as they are actually constituted, an externally poor lifestyle helps to create the interior attitude of poverty: the humble confidence in God demanded of us, and offered to us, by the gift of this Beatitude.

Poverty of spirit, then, and the interior renunciation to which it leads, is a radical, absolute requirement for entering into the kingdom of God and becoming a disciple of Jesus. The material poverty to which it inclines, however, is purely relative. Jesus has not told us *how* to be poor in our concrete lives or in the life of the church down through history. This "how" must be the object of an ongoing search on our part. However, we can sketch certain criteria for recognizing our own concrete lifestyle of poverty:

1. Poverty is a personal grace and call. Each Christian community and each individual Christian must continually search for the particular form of poverty to which God calls that group or that person. There are no recipes here. Poverty is most circumstantial. It varies with one's education, particular culture, society, position in that society, employment, physical and mental health, and so on. Poverty must humanize and liberate, interiorly, and the nature of this humanization and liberation will vary from group to group and individual to individual. What may be a liberating form of detachment for one person or group may be a source of tension and interior oppression for others. It frequently requires a good deal of time to perceive what particular style of poverty God is asking of a particular Christian or community of Christians. It is in prayer that God will reveal the road to poverty, and the road will be an arduous one. Ultimately, poverty is a grace, a gift of God.

2. Poverty is dynamic. It keeps on creating new expressions

and new demands, according to new circumstances and new challenges. One is not allowed to ensconce oneself in the cozy framework of a static, casuistical "poverty acquired." Poverty is never "acquired." Poverty is never summed up in a formula. In each new life situation—indeed, day by day even in the same situation—we must be constantly updating our response to new forms of Jesus' call to "give up all our possessions" and follow him.

3. Poverty is historical. It must maintain intimate ties with the poverty of the sociologically poor and the requirements of their liberation. It is not only the external expressions of poverty that change and develop down through the ages. The Christian motivations and historical significance of poverty also undergo an evolution in the course of time. The motives and style of the poverty of the medieval saints is no longer adequate today. What may well have been an acceptable "witness of poverty" in communities of the church in times gone by is acceptable no longer.

Concretely the historical form of poverty today must be coherent with Christian solidarity, with predilection for the poor and oppressed. It is no longer possible to concretize one's particular option of evangelical poverty in the absence of all reference to the actual poor and needy, apart from any inspiration in them and their lot. Theirs, after all, is the only real, sociological poverty that exists, and voluntary, evangelical poverty will have a meaning only if it partakes of, and resembles, the actual poverty of the poor.

In accordance with each one's particular call, evangelical poverty will necessarily lead its practitioner to an option for the poor. It will lead him or her to a sharing of their perspective and their liberation. It will lead to a commitment to justice, with all the risks and consequences of such a commitment. To be evangelically poor in our social context today will be to identify the poor and their cause.

Thus the "first Beatitudes" of Luke and Matthew converge. Matthew gives us the mystique—the spirituality—and the needed freedom to be faithful, individually and as church, to the kingdom, which (as Luke shows us) privileges the poor and makes its option for them. Poverty of spirit is the Christian attitude that animates poverty as commitment to the poor.

4. Hence Christian poverty is not expressed only in a lack of, and detachment from, money and material goods. There are other expressions of poverty and interior liberty. Detachment from prestige, detachment in the face of criticism, detachment from power in its various forms, detachment from the need to "have a career," detachment in the face of risks, insecurity, persecution—these are a few of the many forms of poverty to which God calls the Christian, and especially the apostle, in the various stages of his or her missionary venture. The poor are the ones whose hearts are set on the values of the kingdom. They are the ones who have humbly and confidently abandoned themselves into the hands of God.

5. Poverty is a function of evangelization, and as such is inseparable from it. We shall see more on this point later.

Let us return to the central message of the first two Matthean Beatitudes. These Beatitudes express a demand on the Christian in terms of his or her attitude. Hence they are also a portrait of Jesus himself. In him alone are these Beatitudes perfectly realized. He is the sole model of "poverty of spirit" and "gentleness." He himself revealed this to his disciples explicitly, for this is an essential trait of his spirituality. "Come to me," he said, "all you who labor and are overburdened, and I will give you rest. Shoulder my yoke and learn from me, for I am gentle and humble in heart, and you will find rest for your souls. Yes, my yoke is easy and my burden light" (Mt. 11:28–30). Besides revealing who Jesus is, these words repeat the promise of happiness made to those who imitate Christ in his gentleness and his poverty of spirit: they will find the yoke of Christ a light one, and will share in the goods of the kingdom that God has hidden from the "learned and the clever" and revealed "to mere children"—the poor and the simple (cf. Mt. 11:25).

The prophetic tradition corroborates Jesus' attitude of gentleness and humility of spirit, approaching it from the perspective of his mission. Matthew cites Isaiah in order to convey to us Jesus' evangelistic style, the style that inspires and permeates these first two Matthean Beatitudes:

He will not brawl or shout,
nor will anyone hear his voice in the streets.
He will not break the crushed reed,
nor put out the smouldering wick
till he has led the truth to victory . . . [Mt. 12:19-20].

This brings us to poverty of spirit as an attitude and demand of
evangelization.

Poverty in Evangelization

Evangelical poverty—that is, interior liberty as expressed in a
concrete individual and social lifestyle—is essential if evangelization is to be Christian. Evangelization is actually conditioned
on poverty as understood in this sense. In the spiritual doctrine
of Matthew's Beatitudes, this is the all-encompassing disposition
of heart that colors all other prerequisites for identification with
Jesus the Happy One and Jesus the Evangelizer.

Our reflection has been leading us to consider the meaning
and importance that poverty of spirit holds for evangelization as
well as for the spirituality of the evangelizer and the evangelizing
Christian community. Let us now gather together what we have
seen about the relationship between poverty and evangelization.

To evangelize is to proclaim and promote the values of the
kingdom according to the message of Jesus. These values are
synthesized in the Beatitudes. We know that they are present
reality, that they must constantly grow, in individuals as in society, and that they are to reach the fullness of their liberating
and beatifying power in eternal life. There is a basic dimension
in the values of the kingdom that is not seen but hoped for. The
preaching of values to be hoped for is an essential of evangelization. But it must be a preaching in more than just words; one
must "preach" in attitude as well, and in a lifestyle that testifies
to trust in God and his promises for the future.

Poverty is the testimony of filial trust. Freedom and detachment from things, persons, power, wealth, and so on bear witness that the God we preach is reality, that he is capable of satis-
fying human life and longings to the full, and that the values of
the kingdom, lived in the present in a spirit of hope, are superior

to the values of earth. The evangelizing church renders itself credible in its members when it causes to shine forth in them, in poverty, the higher values it preaches.

To evangelize is to make an option for the poor, in accordance with the doctrine propounded to us by Luke. This option implies a preferential identification with the poor and the oppressed and with their just cause. But the option and the identification will be authentic and credible only if we share with those with whom we seek to identify. The proof of identification for love's sake is sharing. And we must share not only our liberation projects, but our lifestyle, our social condition—in a word, our poverty. Thus the apostle's voluntary poverty springs from his or her sincere love for the poor, which creates in him or her the necessary conditions for evangelizing as Jesus did—Jesus who "became poor for your sake [that is, for love of the poor], to make you rich out of his poverty" (2 Cor. 8:9).

Evangelization must conform to the attitude of Jesus, who was "gentle and humble of heart" (Mt. 11:29), who "will not break the crushed reed, nor put out the smouldering wick," who "will not brawl or shout, nor will anyone hear his voice in the streets" (Mt. 12:19-20)—that is, the evangelizer must respect each individual person, refuse to force herself or himself upon anyone, and recognize truth and good wherever they are found. But if it is to achieve this conformity, evangelization will have to bear the stamp of humility, respect, and self-abnegation. The credibility of the message itself will require this step, as will its acceptance by those who hear it.

The basis for this attitude is in the Beatitudes of poverty of spirit and gentleness, which inspire in us this style of humble, patient, respectful evangelization.

Evangelization requires a means of action; hence, goods and money. In this respect as well, the church is called upon to bear witness to an important aspect of poverty: the evangelical use of wealth in the service of the kingdom, according to criteria for using goods and money in ways that will be worthy of that kingdom.

Even if it disposes of great sums of money, huge resources, and all the effective modern means of furthering the apostolate, the church must still bear witness to poverty. This poses grave

problems for the institutional poverty of the church at the
present time. The extent, the challenges, and the complexity of
evangelization in modern society require ever more costly means
and methods of missionary activity, and call for the manage-
ment and disposition of great sums by church institutions.

At the same time, the church's wealth maintains its radical
ambiguity, its penchant for becoming lord and master, as Christ
warned in the Sermon on the Mount (cf. Mt. 6:24). The Christian community can transform itself into a source of power,
greed, and injustice. Wealth in the church also has need of an
ongoing evangelization.

The church is radically poor in its evangelical ideal. Its only
riches are Christ and the mission it has received from him. It has
no other "possession" but the apostolate, and the means necessary for engaging in it. This is the only justification for money in
the church. Only the apostolate as a ministry of reconciliation
can redeem the possession and use of money in the church.

In modern pastoral practice, the question of the church's
poverty cannot be simplistically posed in terms of "having" or
"not having." The question must be put at a deeper and more
demanding level. Nor can it be posed in terms of "economy."
Economizing in the face of the challenges of God's kingdom is
not always poverty. In the church it can be acquisitiveness,
greed. The apostolate is not in the service of money; money is in
the service of the apostolate. "You cannot be the slave both of
God and of money" (Mt. 6:24). One evangelical and pastoral
criterion for the use of money in the church is whether or not the
first consideration in its possession and disposition is the good
of the kingdom and the will of Christ. If it is, then we must
spend everything necessary. If we give priority to the glory of
God and the good of others, generous spending can then be a
form of poverty; for, in the church, money is the Lord's. This is
Jesus' lesson to Judas in Bethany, where the woman with the
alabaster jar of nard anointed the Lord's feet (cf. Mk. 14:3-9).
Ostensibly Judas was concerned with the "waste" of the precious stuff, whereas in his heart of hearts what vexed him was
the lost opportunity for a profitable investment.

What criteria do we have, then, for reconciling poverty and
the use of money, frequently large sums of it, in the apostolate,

for reconciling the possession of resources in the service of the kingdom with the obligation we have to "redeem" such wealth?

The Christian community must face this question, without preconceptions, in every place and age. The problem of money in the apostolate must not be swept under the carpet. We must recognize that the problem exists, and endeavor to resolve it on gospel principles.

First of all the church will be offering a witness to poverty by making the same request of the members of its own community, rich and poor, as well as of the local churches (which can also be rich or poor), that it makes of all humanity: to do justice, to share with one another "what earth has given and human hands have made." The church will function as a leaven of reconciliation and of solidarity when its own communities can furnish the world with realistic models of communion in the goods they possess, along with a right appreciation of the value of poor and humble toil.

This writer believes that the apostolate, while having need of the resources necessary for growth and development, ought to maintain an institutional lifestyle that will serve as a witness to the evangelical power of "poor means." After all, the church is not just a society possessing and managing financial resources. It is the community that proclaims the Beatitudes.

The witness of "poor means" in the apostolate will consist primarily in paying full attention to the warning of the word of God that we cannot serve two masters (cf. Mt. 6:24). The sole agent of the apostolate is Christ, and all natural means must be seen in relationship to his grace. The church places its trust in Christ alone, not in material resources; for it knows that the ultimate effect of evangelization is not brought about by "means" and "resources" at all.

In its concrete attitudes, as in its criteria and all its decisions, the Christian community should offer witness to its reliance, above and beyond any material resources it may have at its disposal, on the force of the word of the gospel, on charity, and on a commitment to justice, poverty, prayer, and the cross. It knows that "all these other things will be given you as well" (Mt. 6:33). The deepest expression of its belief in Jesus and his promise will be not to "worry" about riches, for the "Father knows you need them all. Set your hearts on his kingdom first, and on his righteousness" (Mt. 6:31–33).

The testimony of "poor means" in the apostolate will prevent us from thinking that we "cannot do anything" because we "lack the financial resources." It will free us from the notion that money is a condition for the profound efficacy of mission. Not only is this attitude incorrect from the point of view of the gospel, it is also, at least in Latin America, belied by pastoral experience. Very often it is the poorest dioceses and churches that are the most dynamic, the most missionary, and most favored with the trust of the people. By contrast, many apostolic endeavors that are pastorally effective in their beginnings, while they still seek a radical fidelity to the criteria of the gospel for the application of "poor means," fall away from their first effectiveness, or even become corrupt with respect to their original objectives when they grow wealthy and begin to develop material means of pastoral activity.

An apostolic style characterized by "poor means" demands that these means be selected and applied in solidarity with the message being proclaimed as well as with the milieu in which it is proclaimed. If the resources being brought to bear on the work of evangelization contrast with the content of that evangelization—the Beatitudes—and with the condition of the poor who are to be the beneficiaries of that evangelization, then this is the "rich" missionary style, and we are rich missionaries. We are using affluence to "bring the message to the people." We shall see the message grow nebulous and rhetorical. The people will no longer grasp it, for they will no longer experience it as relevant to themselves and their condition. The gospel doesn't "get through." The gospel doesn't work. In the apostolate, method cannot be divorced from content. For in the apostolate, the means of transmission condition the credibility of the message. We cannot credibly proclaim the Beatitudes with means and resources that contradict the Beatitudes. We cannot address ourselves to the poor with a style and method that are altogether foreign to their lifestyle and that categorize us as belonging to the world of the wealthy.

As a consequence, evangelization, whether addressed to rich or poor, whether carried on with abundant resources or scant, if it is to bear rich and lasting fruit in terms of liberation of the poor and the conversion of the rich, must always be carried on from a point of departure among the poor—from "their side," as it were. Not that one must necessarily go first among the poor and there establish a physical base, or headquarters, from which to move out to evangelize. But one must always move from a *stance* of solidarity with and choice for the cause of justice— which, in Latin America, means the cause of the poor. This is what ultimately determines which "means" are "poor." This is what redeems the use of money in the apostolate, and renders credible, to rich and poor alike, the teaching of the church on the acquisition, possession, and use of wealth.

6

PASSION FOR GOD'S KINGDOM

Happy those who mourn:
they shall be comforted.
Happy those who hunger and thirst for what is right:
they shall be satisfied [Mt. 5:5-6].

The third and fourth Matthean Beatitudes are similar in their content and message. "Those who mourn," or are afflicted, are those who desire the coming of the kingdom so intensely that its delay afflicts them, causes them to suffer. Let us not forget that Matthew is dealing with evangelical attitudes. It was Luke who considered affliction and suffering as part of the human condition.

This attitude of ardent, painful longing for the kingdom is, once more, both a grace and a demand of Jesus. It is identical with the "hunger and thirst for what is right." For, after all, "what is right," or justice, is a quality and earmark of the kingdom. Jesus is speaking of justice here in the biblical sense of the word, where it has a broader and deeper meaning than simply "social justice" in various human relationships. In biblical language, the word used here certainly includes historical, social justice, but it does not specifically denote it.

Justice and "the just," in the Bible and of course in the Beatitudes, denote what actually happens when the kingdom of Christ becomes reality. As a demand on the disciple, "justice" is

45

the acceptance of, and fidelity to, this kingdom and its requirements as manifested in Jesus Christ. In terms of Christian spirituality, justice is holiness. The just one is the saint. Later on
Matthew will place this explicitly on the lips of Jesus:

> If your virtue [*dikaiosúnē*, or biblical "justice"] goes no
> deeper than that of the scribes and Pharisees, you will never
> get into the kingdom of heaven. . . . Set you hearts on his
> kingdom first, and on his righteousness [*dikaiosúnēn*], and all
> these other things will be given to you as well[Mt. 5:20; 6:33].

Here "justice" clearly refers to the kingdom and to the demands
of fidelity to that kingdom, which, of course, constitute holiness.

The justice and holiness of the kingdom, both as grace and as
requirement, begins with a conversion of heart, a personal
change, and ends in the fullness of love and the freedom of
Christ. It constitutes interior liberation, for it expels selfishness
and the slavery, the blindness, of sin. Thus we are taught that
the kingdom of God begins from within us (Lk. 17:21), that we
must be reborn to new life (Jn. 3:3), that those who lose their life
of injustice and sin will find it transformed into a life according
to the kingdom (Mt. 16:25), that the grain of wheat must die in
order to bear the fruit of holiness (Jn. 12:24), and so on.

But the holiness and justice of the kingdom has a social dimension as well. All human realities must be redeemed, and all
human longings and aspirations satisfied, "so that God may be
all in all" (1 Cor. 15:28). Christ has come and laid down his life
so that the values of the kingdom may penetrate not only individuals, but also the family, the economy, culture, politics—
every social relationship. This assertion is a commonplace in the
church's teaching and holds a special relevance wherever a society is scandalously unjust and distant from the ideals of the
kingdom and its holiness.

Where social sinfulness is in the ascendancy, and the influence
of the law of Christ in retreat before it, there a biblical justice
will call for social justice more than elsewhere and assign it privileged attention. In such a case—as in Latin America—the affliction and the hunger and thirst for the kingdom that Jesus asks of

his followers will have strong overtones of longing for social justice and the liberation of the poor and the oppressed. Here biblical justice will demand a struggle for a better society, one more faithful to the values of the kingdom—in other words, a holier society.

The church, too, is insistent with us that the building up of the kingdom of God is inseparable from toil for justice and that Christian holiness demands service to the poor and commitment to their integral liberation. And this is what the third and fourth Matthean Beatitudes inculcate.

The promise of these Beatitudes is equally significant: satiation, consolation. The more intensely the addressees of these Beatitudes desire the coming of the kingdom, the more quickly and more fully will that kingdom come, for them as well as for others. One finds God in proportion as one desires him. The kingdom is built up in the measure that we thirst for its coming. The path to holiness begins with the desire to be holy. Social justice makes its advances to the extent that human beings ardently and efficaciously wish for those advances.

This is revealed to us in the basic revelation that holiness, the values of the kingdom, liberation, and justice in the world are all presented in the form of something promised. They are a gift of God, a grace. They are not merely the result of human efforts and commitments, however effective and well intentioned these efforts and commitments may be. The kingdom and its holiness are the "implosion" into history of God's free gift of love. Their demands and values are beyond the capacities of the human condition. But for Jesus, a human being is more than just a human being, and this is why we are offered the grace of biblical justice. It is a grace to be desired, to be petitioned, and to be welcomed—in the spirit of the Beatitudes.

Evangelization: Deed of the Spirit

The third and fourth Matthean Beatitudes contain three essential teachings on mission. They present us with three requirements of that spirituality needed in order for evangelization to be specifically Christian.

First, all evangelization must cause human beings to grow in justice, in holiness. Its goal is ever conversion to Jesus Christ and his gospel—as explicit a conversion as may be. Human beings are called to holiness. To evangelize means to produce human beings who are "just" and who in turn will ardently desire the propagation of this justice all about them.

This is an essential dimension of mission, as well as of the Christian community engaged in it. No one can give what he or she does not possess. True, evangelization is a task complete in itself. It comprises various stages of its own, and often must make a long journey before finally arriving at the point where it may transmit its religious message. It is also true that all the concrete deeds of liberation, down through the whole course of history, all solidarity and justice, and any enhancement of cultural values, are inseparably connected with the kingdom and its evangelization. All these things make their contribution to the kingdom. But they are not themselves the kingdom. They do not constitute the kingdom in its proper formality. The kingdom comes where Christ is accepted and followed, where men and women are transformed, interiorly, from sinners to saints to just ones, from a selfish people into the sons and daughters of God and brothers and sisters of one another.

Second, in its most profound dimension, evangelization is the deed of God's Spirit. It is the free grace of God the Father, who, out of love, seeks to transform a sinful and unjust world into the image of his kingdom. Human beings, however inspired and committed, are unequal to a like task. No human activity can cause the kingdom or its justice. Jesus alone brings us the kingdom—Jesus the incarnate and salvific love of God, Jesus who makes the kingdom and its justice possible for us by his life, death, and resurrection.

Evangelization is the act of a God who has sent us his Son and who prospers his deed of evangelization in his church, which, thanks to the Spirit it has received from him, maintains its indissoluble bonds with mission. It is the Spirit dwelling in the church who ultimately converts, who ultimately builds the kingdom, who makes all things new (cf. Rev. 21:5), and who brings justice into the hearts of individuals and their societies. Left to themselves, women and men are incapable of evangelizing. But they know that the results of their efforts far transcend the limits of what the eye can observe. What the Spirit accomplishes in the work of evangelization outstrips all the means of the church and its evangelizers.

The message of the third and fourth Matthean Beatitudes is a message of confidence and hope in the efficacy of mission. To doubt our evangelizing activity is to doubt the effectiveness of the Spirit. Here again Jesus is the model of the Beatitudes. No one is as afflicted, as famished, for the dawning of the justice of the kingdom in our midst as is he. Our zeal and longing are nothing in comparison with the desire and zeal for the coming of the kingdom with which Jesus was eaten up, and which is at work today in the activity of this Spirit in the church.

To evangelize is to identify with the burning desire for justice in the heart of Jesus—Jesus the Happy One, Jesus the Evangelizer. It means surrendering to the missionary movement of his Spirit, in the humble realization that he has ways that are not our ways (Isa. 55:8) and that he breathes where he will (Jn. 3:8).

Third, the mystique or spirituality of the kingdom is a synthesis of three attitudes in tension: ardent desire, a consciousness of one's own limits and powerlessness, and confident hope. These attitudes, when authentic, will cause prayer to well up from within us. Prayer is one of the basic needs of a missionary church. Prayer is the practical recognition of our powerlessness to evangelize, of our conviction that mission is not merely, or even primarily, the implementation of our human means, but the work of the Spirit acting within us. To pray is to open ourselves to God, who fills our narrow limits to overflowing. Prayer is allowing ourselves to be filled up with his justice in order to go and build justice in others. Prayer is cooperation with the liberating action of the Spirit, who works in the roots of people's consciousness and who freely enters where human means cannot penetrate.

The prayer of the evangelizer is the Christian response to the awareness that the kingdom of justice is a gift of God, that it is something to be longed for and begged for. It is a response to the fact that those who toil for the justice of the kingdom must themselves live lives of justice and that justice and holiness come from God and must be received as a grace. "Thy Kingdom come!"

7

THE PATH OF MERCY

Happy the merciful:
they shall have mercy shown them [Mt. 5:7].

Fundamental to Matthew's presentation of the Beatitudes is the fifth, the Beatitude of mercy. For mercy, as we shall see, concerns the attitude and Christian practice of love for our brothers and sisters, which is the quintessence of the following of Christ.

The mercy that Jesus proposes to us is not mere compassion or sympathy. It is solidarity. It is efficacious involvement with our sister and our brother. Let us place this Beatitude in the overall context of Jesus' teaching, as we have done with the other Beatitudes. What precisely does Jesus say about mercy?

We find the paradigm and norm of mercy in the parable of the Good Samaritan (Lk. 10:25-37): " 'Which of these three, do you think, proved himself a neighbor to the man who fell into the brigands' hands?' 'The one who took pity on him [the one who showed him mercy],' he replied. Jesus said to him, 'Go, and do the same yourself' " (vss. 36-37). Similarly in the description of the Last Judgment (Mt. 25:31-46), the blessed of God are those who have practiced charity in action: "Come, you whom my Father has blessed. . . . For I was hungry and you gave me food . . ." (Mt. 25:34-35).

Now we see what mercy is in the gospel. It consists of two things, two aspects: active commitment, or involvement, and forgiveness.

To be merciful, according to the teaching of Christ, means to commit ourselves to aiding the needy and the afflicted. It means going out of ourselves in order to enter into efficacious solidarity with our neighbor in need. Mercy, as an expression of love for our brothers and sisters, must reach out to every form of need, every type of misery, both material and spiritual. For, in the Christian praxis of love, it is the poor in their material misery and sinners in their spiritual misery, who are the privileged recipients of mercy, and hence of evangelization. The two Scripture passages just cited, the one on the Good Samaritan and the other on the Last Judgment, speak to us of mercy to the poor and the oppressed. The parables of the Lost Sheep (Lk. 15:4–7) and the Prodigal Son (Lk. 15:11–32) are about mercy to sinners.

Mercy also means forgiving from the heart our neighbor who has offended us—over and over again if need be ("seventy times seven," that is, an unlimited number of times). The parable of the Unforgiving Debtor (Mt. 18:23–35) explicitly teaches that forgiveness is an essential part of mercy and love for brother and sister: " 'You wicked servant, . . . were you not bound . . . to have pity on your fellow servant just as I had pity on you?' " (vss. 32–33). Thus we see that forgiveness is a basic aspect of solidarity, a fundamental part of the abandonment of our own selfishness in order to go forth to meet our neighbor.

As this Beatitude contains a demand, so also it shares a promise. This double aspect of requirement and promise constitutes the essence of each Matthean Beatitude. Here, in the fifth, the promise of the kingdom (and we know that all the Beatitudes, in both Luke and Matthew, promise the kingdom, under different images) takes the form of the mercy God shows to us. But it is more specific than that; and herein lies the originality of the fifth Beatitude. It conditions God's mercy toward us on our mercy toward others. It conditions God's mercy on our forgiveness and commitment. The fifth Beatitude presents us with the essential condition for obtaining mercy from God, which we must have in order to enter the kingdom.

The relationship between God's mercy toward us and our mercy toward others is a constantly recurring theme in Jesus' preaching. It is in the parable just mentioned, that of the Unforgiving Debtor: "That is how my heavenly Father will deal with you unless you each forgive your brother from your heart"

(Mt. 18:35). Similarly the Letter of James warns: "There will be judgment without mercy for those who have not been merciful themselves" (Jas. 2:13)—echoing the words of Christ in the Sermon on the Mount: "Do not judge, and you will not be judged; because the judgments you give are the judgments you will get, and the amount you measure out is the amount you will be given" (Mt. 7:1-2). Even in the Lord's Prayer we ask God's forgiveness for our offenses "as we have forgiven those who are in debt to us" (Mt. 6:12).

Once more Jesus is the model of the Beatitudes. He is God's limitless mercy, incarnate in our midst. In the Old Testament itself, "mercy" appears as the most meaningful and characteristic trait of the God of Israel in his dealings with his people; we need only glance at any one of the 150 Psalms to be convinced of this. In Jesus Christ, God's decisive revelation of mercy, this is a central trait of his own spirituality and mission. Jesus is the one, sole Merciful One. He poured out his mercy in the midst of his people. His mission was a veritable ministry of mercy, especially among the poor and the sinful. He embodies the Good Shepherd, the father of the Prodigal, and the Good Samaritan as he mercifully "has pity on the crowds" (cf. Mt. 9:36; 14:14; 15:32; Mk. 8:2) and "lays down his life for his friends" (Jn. 15:13). In this Beatitude we are offered the grace, as well as presented with the demand, of sharing in the mercy of Jesus.

In the Service of a Christian Communion of Brothers and Sisters

The Beatitude of mercy contains two essential teachings on evangelization: (1) The objective of evangelization is the building up of a Christian community of brothers and sisters. It is a service rendered to this loving community, inspired by the mystique of mercy. (2) Mercy is the obligatory path to the construction of such a community among all human beings. Solidarity and involvement create this community; forgiveness reestablishes it. Both dimensions of mercy are irreplaceable.

Let us consider these two facets of the spirituality of evangelization in conjunction. The preaching and activity of Jesus has the kingdom of God as its main objective. The anticipation in history of this kingdom to come has been aptly formulated by the church as the communion of human beings with God and with one another (cf. *Lumen Gentium*, no. 1)—that is, as the condition of daughters and sons of God and brothers and sisters of one another, which is the condition that makes this communion Christian. Jesus has revealed to us that God is the Father of all men and women, and has established God's common parenthood of us all as the basis of our intercommunion with one another as sisters and brothers.

By insisting absolutely on brotherly and sisterly love, and by insisting on mercy as both a demand of this love and its bond and seal (Jn. 13:34), and by declaring the second commandment of the law to "resemble" the first (Mt. 22:39; Lk. 10:27; Jn. 15:12), Jesus has made love and mercy, in concrete terms of the intercommunion of sisters and brothers, the sign by which his kingdom may be recognized.

Thus we can validly assert that what Jesus came to accomplish, and actually did accomplish, is the creation of a community of brothers and sisters that presupposes the condition of sons and daughters of God. His dream is to change women and men from selfish persons into sisters and brothers, and divided, unjust groups and societies into just and loving ones. Jesus laid down his life in order to make it possible to build a community of brothers and sisters in the future of the church. Now love can triumph over hate, and justice over injustice, because Christ died and rose again. "When I am lifted up from the earth, I shall draw all men to myself" (Jn. 12:32). For Jesus had to die "not for the nation only, but to gather together in unity the scattered children of God" (Jn. 11:52). "Scattering" is a biblical word for the division, hatred, and rivalry produced by sin. The Tower of Babel is the biblical symbol of the source of this "scattering," and the cross is the sign of the transformation of the "scattering" into a community of sisters and brothers.

The building of this Christian community is the raison d'être of the church and its mission. Human beings' communion with God and with one another is the only adequate measure and criterion for evaluating the church's presence, activity, and institutions among men and women. Evangelization is service rendered to a community of brothers and sisters.

The missionary imperative, incumbent upon the church, to

intervene in "temporal matters"—social, political, economic, and cultural affairs—stems from the relationship such questions necessarily have to a Christian community of brothers and sisters. Jesus' dream is to make sisters and brothers not only of individuals but also of whole societies. Hence his message calls for the implementation of the values of solidarity and love not only among individuals, but in the economy, in politics, in culture. His message likewise calls for the denunciation of economic, political, and cultural systems that destroy, or block, or outlaw a communion of brothers and sisters. Economics—the science of wealth—is not a matter of moral indifference. It is not neutral with respect to the values of the kingdom. Economics either serves human beings or dehumanizes them. It either enhances justice and communion by facilitating the sharing of wealth, or it reinforces injustice and division.

Nor are political institutions—power institutions—indifferent with respect to the gospel of a community of sisters and brothers. The "powers that be" either serve the weakest of the weak and succor the forsaken, thus reestablishing justice and communion in society, or else they further the cause of injustice and division. The same is to be said of cultural institutions, whose function in a just society of brothers and sisters is to propagate knowledge and culture in such a way that it will be accessible to all.

The reason for the social dimension of evangelization, then, is that, in order to create a communion of brothers and sisters in the world, one must deliver that world from its social servitude, from its social sinfulness—as this is expressed in economics, politics, and culture. Evangelization is in the service of liberation, for the purpose of a just society of sisters and brothers.

The problem of a community of sisters and brothers will never be resolved, either for evangelization or, still less, for humanity, until we discover concrete, practical ways to reestablish brotherly and sisterly relationships among ourselves, within our community, and in society as a whole. The state of the question is this: How can we create such a community? How can we make brothers and sisters of one another? Does a common nationality and culture, or a common religion, or geographical proximity, or family ties, or a community of interests produce such a community?

In the Christian perspective, all these natural bonds have their contribution to make to the Christian community we seek. They can all facilitate its construction. But they do not constitute it. It is the fifth Beatitude that gives us the gospel formula for a Christian community of sisters and brothers. Here we read that this community is built essentially on the practice of mercy.

This is the teaching of Jesus himself in the parable of the Good Samaritan (Lk. 10:25-37). There the question arises, "Which . . . proved himself a neighbor to the man who fell into the brigands' hands?" (vs. 36). That is, which of the various protagonists in the story actually created a bond of brotherhood with the victim? And the answer is: "The one who took pity on him" (vs. 37). The Samaritan. Not the priest, and not the Levite—in spite of all the obvious reasons these two had for making themselves the brother of the unfortunate victim, for of course they were of the same ethnic origin, nationality, and religion as he. No, it was the Samaritan—separated from him by religious rivalries and racial tension: "Jews, in fact, do not associate with Samaritans" (Jn. 4:9). He alone managed to make himself the brother of the poor wretch, transcending himself and his prejudices and becoming involved with him in order to liberate him from his misery. The word "pity" in the expression "took pity on him" is the biblical word for "mercy."

Mercy is the bond of Christian community. God does not bestow Christian community upon us ready-made. We are not one another's brothers and sisters automatically, by virtue of some preestablished rationale of solidarity like nationality, physical community, or the like. Brotherhood and sisterhood must be continually created and preserved—by the arduous uses of mercy. One thing alone is incompatible with Christian community: selfishness, the denial of efficacious solidarity and love.

In summoning us to mercy, this Beatitude calls us to the task of becoming one another's sister or brother—the task of creating communion. And at the same time, it calls us to make this task an essential of evangelization.

Mercy is the commandment of brotherly and sisterly love brought to full maturity. As a habitual disposition and attitude it forms part of the spirituality of the evangelizer, the mystique of the disciple of the merciful Christ. Let us summarize the demands of Christian mercy—which are likewise the demands of brotherly and sisterly love—with respect to evangelization.

As part and parcel of the following of Christ, mercy in evangelization will extend special privileges to the two forms of misery to which the Lord himself paid such special attention: the poor and the sinful. In other words, we follow the example of Jesus in privileging those who live in either of two sorts of wretchedness: material wretchedness and spiritual wretchedness. The preferential option for the poor (those "preferred persons" of the gospel) and the search for the "lost sheep," the alienated, the impious, and the corrupt (who are the beneficiaries of redemption), together constitute that project of mercy that is at the very heart of evangelization. Jesus identified with the poor and oppressed, and it was in this identification as his point of departure that he dedicated himself to the conversion of all sinners, poor or not. The categories "poor" and "sinful" are not mutually exclusive, of course. The misery of sin has no respect for social status and crosses over their lines of demarcation most handily. Hence mercy, too, as commitment to liberation from moral evil, will embrace all human beings alike.

Christian mercy is universal. It is undiscriminating. No human being may be excluded from our love, for love commits us to the liberation of all humankind from its material and spiritual misery. This requirement of universal love is marvelously well presented in the parable we have just referred to—the one about the Good Samaritan. Jesus sets before us the mercy shown the victim by the Samaritan as a model of the law of love of neighbor. "Go, and do the same yourself," he commands (Lk. 10:37). In presenting the Samaritan as the one who, by the strength of his love, was able to transcend the prejudices and sectarianism that divided him from the wounded Jew and go to his aid, Jesus is establishing the norm of Christian mercy: to be ready to serve anyone who has need of us along the road of life and become that person's sister or brother, whatever his or her political ideology, social class, or moral condition.

Universal mercy, then, is the driving force in evangelization. It is the test of whether the community of brothers and sisters that evangelization seeks to build is truly a sign of the coming of the kingdom of a God who is merciful Father of all, who "causes his sun to rise on bad men as well as good" (Mt. 5:45).

Christian mercy is actualized in the realism of the concrete world. It sets up a direct relationship with the individual, actual person whom we meet along the road of our life, and who has a right to hope for mercy from us. For the path of mercy is a path of strict realism. Jesus requires that it be so. He spares us the temptation of an abstract, idealistic, "universal" love that neglects the men and women of our immediate vicinity in favor of those at a distance—the temptation to opt for the poor in general, but not for the particular poor who live with us and share our real, everyday society, the temptation of a "missionary concern" for the poor and the sinners of Asia and Africa but not for the ones in our neighborhood, the poor and the sinners who live and work with us.

Christ's mandate to go and build a communion of brothers and sisters is to be carried out in the limited world of *one's own human relationships.* The test of love's maturity is in the exercise of mercy toward the real persons whose faces we see every day.

Christian mercy must have discernible traits. Love is expressed in acts, commitments, deeds, attitudes, and friendship. That "merciful love" not actually directed to a real human being is pure idealism—abstract, interior "intention." It separates two things whose unity is an essential of Christian spirituality: interior attitude and external practice. The traits of a discernible communion of mercy are dictated by mercy's own realism and concretion. The Samaritan "went all the way" in his involvement with the suffering Jew. He employed all human means necessary to help him. He ensured all the attentions his misery had need of.

The commitment of mercy is not an option of love disincarnate. Christian charity includes the perceivable human expression of love and friendship. For love is of its very nature incarnate. This is part and parcel of the spirituality of evangelization. Love never occurs chemically pure. It never occurs in isolation from its concrete expressions. "Purity of intention" and "good will" are beside the point. Love demands the development of one's temperament. Love demands character formation. After all, concrete love goes clothed in values and shortcomings—the values and shortcomings of this or that particular individual who is engaged in its practice.

It is not always the vices of enmity, jealousy, or selfishness that paralyze Christian communion. Very often it is the short-comings that spring from poor character training. After all, love's vehicle of expression is character. The fact that our failings may not be serious ones, or deliberate, does not exempt us from the obligation to put forth an effort to overcome them. Love wears a human face. This is why human failings are detrimental to communion. Poor character formation can result in a temperament that is so preoccupied and distracted, or so timid, that the dynamism of mercy is paralyzed. We can wound others without even knowing it, by our preoccupation or other faults of temperament that have a bearing on charity.

There is a secret place deep within us where our temperament meshes with a certain unconscious selfishness. We all carry this still, dark place about with us. But we have no right to allow it to remain safe and secure, hidden in total darkness. An evangelizer has no right to certain forms of timidity, distraction, aggressiveness, certain complexes or other character faults that interfere with evangelization. The grace of mercy must be allowed to shape and mold our own temperament, even at the more or less unconscious levels of our life where we harbor prejudices, sectarianism, and other antipathies. True, only in heaven will we attain to charity's perfection. Only there will our communion of brothers and sisters be without blemish. For now, this charity and this communion are necessarily precarious and limited. What the Beatitude of mercy asks is that Christ always find us at work struggling to improve the quality of our brotherly and sisterly love.

The Gospel of Forgiveness

The mercy of commitment, as we have seen, is not enough. Alone, it cannot create and preserve a human community of brothers and sisters. Communion is precarious. It is constantly threatened by our failings and shortcomings. Our mercy falls short. Communion is always in the process of being created and destroyed. Christ's communion always needs consolidation, recovery, and rebuilding; deliberate offenses, prejudices, and injustices weaken and debilitate it.

Mercy in the form of the forgiveness of offenses is the other face of brotherly and sisterly love. Forgiveness is the aspect of mercy that prevents resentment and division from paralyzing intercommunion. Just as it is the task of mercy-as-commitment to go out to those in need and build a community of sisters and brothers, so it belongs to mercy-as-forgiveness, or mutual pardon, to rebuild and consolidate that community as often as need be.

Evangelization is a proclamation of forgiveness, and education in forgiveness. It proclaims the limitless pardon of God and transmits God's demand that we pardon our sisters and brothers as well. Even were they to offend us "seventy times seven," we are to forgive them without end. Evangelization is at once a service of communion and a service of reconciliation through forgiveness.

Jesus' mission is a mission of liberation from misery and a mission of reconciliation. These are the two faces of mercy, two aspects of one and the same deed of consolidation and Christian community. They are inseparable. The consolidation of a Christian community of brothers and sisters is a labor in the cause of peace; indeed it brings peace, for wherever we find consolidated communion, we find authentic peace as well.

8

THE CALL TO EXPERIENCE GOD

Happy the pure in heart:
they shall see God [Mt. 5:8].

Our journey through the Beatitudes in Matthew has led us at last to the mountaintop of Christian perfection. The arduous ascent began with poverty of spirit; now it culminates in purity of heart. And the path we have followed constitutes both the spirituality of evangelization and a portrait of Jesus, our God made flesh.

The sixth Beatitude speaks to us of the "pure in heart." The ever recurring promise of the kingdom is here formulated in new terms: the "vision of God." This Beatitude is inspired by the language of the prophets and the Psalms, especially Psalm 24, where nearness to God and intimacy with him are promised to those "whose hands are clean, whose heart is pure" (Ps. 24:4a).

What does "purity of heart" mean in the Bible? Obviously it goes well beyond the virtue of purity, or chastity of heart, although it of course includes that. To be pure of heart means to have a genuine interior life in conformity with the law of God. More precisely, the "pure in heart" are those who are unflagging in their efforts to uproot all deceit from their hearts, along with any other evil tendencies that may lurk there. They are those who have purified themselves of the worship of idols,

60

"whose soul does not pay homage to worthless things" (Ps. 24:4b), in the form of distortions and deformations of the one true God. This Beatitude furnishes us with a synthesis of all the attitudes and requirements of the others. It demands the radical excision of all idolatry from our hearts (cf. Pss. 15; 24).

Implicit in purity of heart, of course, is "clean hands." In the gospel ethic, a "pure heart" and "clean hands" are two inseparable facets of one and the same purity. A "pure heart" is an interior disposition; "clean hands" are works and deeds consistent with this interior disposition. A person who refuses to worship idols in his or her heart will not go in pursuit of them in everyday life. In emphasizing interior purity in this Beatitude, Matthew is directing attention to the origin of all holiness and placing Christ's disciples on their guard against formalism or pharisaical moral casuistry. After all, this was the constant preoccupation of Jesus himself, all during his ministry.

> You will be able to tell them by their fruits. . . . A sound tree cannot bear bad fruit, nor a rotten tree bear good fruit. . . . You who clean the outside of cup and dish and leave the inside full of extortion and intemperance. Blind Pharisee! Clean the inside of cup and dish first so that the outside may become clean as well [Mt. 7:16, 18; 23:25-26].

But what is most surprising in this Beatitude is its promise: "They shall see God." Those who have delivered themselves from idols are promised the vision of God. Or rather, since the human heart perpetually renews its idols: in the degree that we overcome our idols, in that degree we shall attain a clearer vision of God.

The promise is a most unusual one. In biblical tradition no one can see God (1 Jn. 4:12), or no one can see the face of God and live (Exod. 33:19). The great theophanies of the Old Testament never go so far as to render God himself visible. Moses only saw God's "back" (Exod. 33:23). Elijah saw God, but then was snatched up to heaven in a whirlwind (2 Kings 2:11). And yet in this Beatitude Jesus promises his disciples the vision of God—a genuine sight of the true God himself:

If you know me, you know my Father too.
From this moment you know him and have seen him.
. . . To have seen me is to have seen the Father. . . .
And eternal life is this:
to know you,
the only true God,
and Jesus Christ whom you have sent [Jn. 14:7, 9; 17:3].

Then what can this mean, the sight of God, the vision of God? First, we know that God has promised us a vision of himself after death, in eternal life. "Then we shall be seeing face to face. . . . Then I shall know as fully as I am known" (1 Cor. 13:12–13). Here Paul is speaking of complete union with God in heaven, the full vision of God. There, to have sight of God will mean to enter into the inexhaustible fullness of an intimate life and happiness that will fulfill our human destiny in a manner beyond all imagining—in "things that no eye has seen and no ear has heard, things beyond the mind of man, all that God has prepared for those who love him" (1 Cor. 2:9; cf. Isa. 64:3).

This vision of God—which coincides with the fulfillment of all our human needs and strivings, and indeed ineffably exceeds them (for a human being is more than a human being)—is, to be sure, the eschatological kingdom of God, whose promise and realization underlie all the Beatitudes. But what is novel and astonishing in the sixth Beatitude is that this vision of God is offered, to those who toil to keep their "heart pure" and their "hands clean," in the present, in the here and now. For the disciples of Jesus, the vision of God has already begun. And it is an authentic vision of the true face of God—albeit in precarious and limited wise, like any promise of the kingdom anticipated in the here and now.

Once more we are proposed a share in the experience of Jesus, the Happy One. This time it is a share in his experience of absolute purity of heart and total immersion in the vision of his Father. We share in this vision as a gift—the freest of all the gifts bestowed on the daughters and sons of God—in the measure that we prepare ourselves for it by purity of heart. Actually, of course, purity of heart is itself a gift of God, so that the purification of our heart is something to be received and accepted from him:

> I shall pour clean water over you and you will be cleansed; I shall cleanse you of all your defilement and all your idols. I shall give you a new heart, and put a new spirit in you; I shall remove the heart of stone from your bodies and give you a heart of flesh instead. I shall put my spirit in you, and make you keep my laws and sincerely respect my observances [Ezek. 36:25–27].

But what can it mean to see God on this earth? God cannot be seen with the eyes of flesh. He can, however, be "experienced" with the eyes of faith. The vision of God on earth is the experience of God in faith. The depth of this experience will be in proportion to the vitality of one's faith and the love to which that faith is joined. It is genuine experience, for faith and love are "antennae" that the human being possesses for receiving the revelation of a God who seeks to communicate himself as he is. At the same time it is a limited, obscure experience—as is the light of faith that produces it.

To see God is to experience him in the reality of our life, however wrapped in clouds that faith can pierce only a little. The experience of God is the living conviction we feel in the depths of our spirit, where sensation and pure reason cannot penetrate, that the God of Jesus-alive is present, at this very moment, within us, within others, and within history, and that this presence of his is merciful, liberating love. To experience God is to know, existentially and viscerally, that we are in his hands.

The experience of God is nothing other than the fruit of Christian contemplation. The grace of the vision of God is the grace of contemplation. We are dealing with the "contemplatives' Beatitude" here. The contemplative is a person who has a living experience of the God of Jesus. Hence the contemplative is also a person who, through the experience of the absolute God, is continually emptying his or her soul of idols. For, just as the contemplative experience of God constantly purifies our heart, so also purity of heart constantly prepares the contemplative for the living experience of the God of Jesus.

The demand and the promise of the sixth Beatitude reinforce each other, deep within God's call to contemplate him and be delivered from our idols. In inviting us to contemplation here on earth, Jesus is calling us to experience himself as the font of all holiness and the motive force of all evangelization.

The sixth Matthean Beatitude, then, is the pinnacle of the missioner's spiritual journey. For it joins evangelization to contemplation and finds in the latter the supreme inspiration of mission.

The Path of Christian Contemplation — *Keeping mind on God*

The grace of the sixth Beatitude calls us to Christian contemplation. What is the nature, and what are the demands, of this contemplation? We are speaking of *Christian* contemplation—not of contemplation, even religious contemplation, in general. "Christian" refers to Christ and the following of Christ. The humanity of Jesus enjoyed the living experience of the contemplation of his Father; hence, to be a "contemplative Christian" means to follow Jesus and share that contemplative path. Our own contemplative experience is not autonomous. It incorporates us into the contemplative Christ. In him we discover the nature and meaning of our own contemplation. Christian contemplation has no meaning apart from the perspective of a contemplative Jesus, for this perspective will indicate the great differences that obtain between the experience of the Christian God and other religious experiences.

Christian contemplation is the experience of the God of Jesus. It is not the experience of an abstract "God," however religious an experience this might be, but of the one, living God revealed to us in Jesus—a God who bestows himself upon us, a God who communicates with women and men in a real way, a God to whom they can surrender by their charity, and a God whom they can know by their faith.

The experience of the living God sounds the death knell for the false gods—the idols—within us. It purifies our hearts and cleanses our hands. The experience of the Christian God is the destruction of selfishness: it transcends any religious experience that might satisfy our "religious sentiment," which asks no questions, and which therefore will fail to produce a radical and continuing change in our life orientation.

The path of Christian contemplation is the relentless road of death to the "old self" (Eph. 4:22; Col. 3:9)—the selfish, idolatrous, human being within us—and our rebirth as disciples and followers of Jesus in the spirit of the Beatitudes.

The experience of the Christian God is obscure—not because God is obscure, but, quite the contrary, because God is Light of light, the very source of all light. It is precisely God's brightness that renders dim all authentic contemplation of him. A human being is incapable of the direct contemplation of God. We are not adapted to such a direct vision, for his "home is inaccessible light" (1 Tim. 6:16), a light connatural to him but impenetrable to us. Our earthly condition is suited to "seeing" not the Light as it is in itself, but as it is reflected in creation. Our human experience, our sensibility, our intelligence enable us to see but flashes of that Pure Light—flashes of the truth, flashes of goodness, beauty, happiness, and fullness. These alone constitute the human medium of our contemplation of God.

And yet Jesus offers us the grace to contemplate God as he is in himself. He invites us to contemplate Light, Goodness, and Truth at their very source, and in their fullness. Through Jesus we have access to a God who is inaccessible in any other way. In granting us his Spirit, Jesus develops within us the capacity for an experience of God "face to face" (1 Cor. 13:12). This capacity, this faculty is our faith life. The life of faith is the only way we have, in our earthly condition, of contemplating God as he is—and not only flashes of him in his world. The eyes of faith adapt to the "inaccessible light"; but of course at the same time, since faith transcends pure reason and sensation, the contemplation of God that our faith-life offers us remains, in comparison with our habitual mode of experience, dim and obscure. The experience of God blinds us. And so, from our side, it "registers" as something dim itself. Our contemplation is made bright by the life of faith (and only by the life of faith). And yet, of its very nature, the conviction and experience that this faith arouses transcends our sensibility and blinds it.

Let us take an analogy from everyday life. Our sense of sight is not made for seeing the sun directly, even though the sun bathes our planet in light. We see sunlight *on* things, however, very well: we see it on persons, things, and the landscape. We could make the mistake of thinking that all these things are "visible" in their own right, visible in themselves. We could forget that they do not possess this quality of themselves, that they do not have the light by which we see them as their own, that it comes to them from the sun. But then the sun sets, and darkness comes upon us. And all at once all these "visible things" become quite invisible!

Then, quite the other way, if we wish to see the sun itself, we must take account of the fact that our eyes are ill-accommodated to this, and that looking straight at the sun with eyes wide open would blind us. So we squint. Thus, and only thus, in the shadow of our own eyelids, so to speak, do we directly experience the light of the sun. When it "gets dark" in our own eyes, the sun is suddenly accessible to us.

It is somewhat the same with the contemplation of God. This is why the great contemplatives and mystics compare it to "night"—to the rupture of our habitual mode of experience. Saint John of the Cross is the outstanding example. In the mystics, the life of faith is called the "brilliant night": "night" because it obscures our ordinary experience; but "brilliant" because it is in this obscurity that we attain to the true Light. We are made to "see God"—to see the Source and Font of life—but in the dark.

The experience of God is historical; and herein it departs from all non-Christian forms of contemplation. By "historical" we mean that we are called to experience God not only in moments of prayer (understanding prayer as contemplation par excellence, by which we relate to God in a unique and privileged manner), but also in life, in action, in nature, and in history. The God of Jesus reveals himself in the heart of each person; but he reveals himself in historical reality as well. Christian contemplation is the experience of the love of a God who seeks to bring his kingdom to realization in us, in our neighbor, and in society. His love manifests itself in history, and impels us to renew that history, by renewing ourselves, our neighbor, and our society. The experience of God in the reality of life is subject to the same conditions as the experience of him in prayer. This experience too is obscure, and presupposes the life of faith. Human experience tells us that to be able to "read" the presence of God's love in the occurrences of life is, of itself, a disconcerting ability with which to be blessed. We do not know the ultimate design of God for individual persons, for the events of life, or for history. Indeed, in relation to the love and the kingdom of God, reality is maimed and shadowy: it is filled with sin, selfishness, sensuality, injustice. At first view, the God of history makes us uncomfortable. We feel a "silence of God" that frightens us. Indeed, reality is at once God's presence and his absence.

Hence the obscurity, from our side, of the presence of God in history. We are not prepared to interpret and decipher everything that happens according to the key of God's love. We believe in this liberating love, we welcome it in our Christian contemplation of reality—but we believe in it and we welcome it in the "brilliant night" of faith. Never do we grasp God wholly; but in this blinding light, we learn to experience him in the various modes of his presence—in the human and evangelical values that we always find present in history. At the same time we gradually learn to experience him in his absences—in hatred, sin, selfishness, and corruption—for the negative, inhuman aspect of reality thrusts us in God's direction too, on account of his very absence there. It generates a special, nostalgic longing for him. Evil is the privation of God. Evil is what happens when God is rejected. Thus evil actually becomes an experience of the love of God, the love of an absent God.

The contemplative experience as a pilgrimage of the presence and absence of God, in the half-light of faith, is another essential of the teaching of the Christian mystics. God at once present and absent, God at once day and night for us, is "connatural" to Christian contemplation, as we bathe in the experience of him both in the face-to-face encounter of contemplation and in the reality of life.

The Christian experience of God occurs in two basic "places." One is in the person of Jesus Christ, contemplated in prayer. The other is in our neighbor. But an encounter with either provides us with an experience of Christ. For, "in so far as you did this to one of the least of these brothers of mine, you did it to me" (Mt. 25:40).

These two ways of meeting, of "seeing" God correspond to the twofold dimension of Christian love. "You must love the Lord your God with all your heart, with all your soul, and with all your mind. This is the greatest and the first commandment. The second resembles it: You must love your neighbor as yourself" (Mt. 22:37; cf. Mk. 12:30; Lk. 10:27).

They likewise correspond to the two ways in which, according to the gospel, Jesus reveals himself to us: "In so far as you did it to one of the least of these brothers of mine, you did it to me. . . . I am the Way, the Truth and the Life. . . . Anyone who says, 'I love God,' and hates his brother, is a liar, since a man who does not love the brother that he can see cannot love God, whom he has never seen" (Mt. 25:40; cf. Jn. 14:6; 1 Jn. 4:20).

The call to experience God is a call to grow in friendship with Jesus in prayer and to surrender. It is also a call to learn to be in the service of a communion of sisters and brothers. Unless we respond to both calls, and seek a synthesis between them, there will be no authentic Christianity, and no experience of contemplation. In Christian contemplation, these experiences are not merely linked; they reinforce each other. Each is verified in the other.

Indeed they are not even actually two experiences. There are no two distinct experiences of God in Christian spirituality. It is the one God of Jesus that we experience in prayer, and in our sister or brother. The God of private prayer and of the Eucharist is the same God who is revealed in the struggle for the rights of the poor and the works of mercy. Hence to plumb the depths of God in prayer is to strengthen our commitment to our brother or sister; and this commitment in turn fosters the continuous purification of the experience of Jesus in prayer.

Mission, mercy, and the service of the poor (and of all our sisters and brothers), as a human and as a missionary experience, ought to be a place where we discover God and become more familiar with the face of Christ. The Spirit of God is revealed in the values of dedication and service, in aspirations of justice and solidarity, in anyone's conversion, in the "least" ones, the suffering, and the needy—everywhere in our neighbor. Human realities and cultures are shot through with the presence of the Spirit and the action of God building his kingdom. They offer us the actual experience of God himself. This is the contemplative dimension of mission. This is what it means to be a "contemplative in action."

And yet this commitment is not enough. It is an inadequate response to the invitation to "see God." Seeing God also requires an exclusive encounter with God's very person, in prayer, in the word, and in the sacraments—that is, in the celebration of the faith. The experience of God in prayer is still the privileged path of Christian contemplation.

The reasons for this are two in particular. First, the human being's vocation to "see God" while still on earth is a call to contemplate him as he is in himself (however dimly), with all the intensity possible to the human condition. In activity we experience God through what is not God. In prayer we experience God without intermediaries, in the exclusivity of the faith encounter. Prayer is an (obscure) face-to-face vision of God.

The second reason why prayer is critical to the Christian experience is that human reality, our neighbor, and the poor fail to constitute a univalent, unambiguous revelation of God. They reveal to us something about God, yes; but they also "reveal" sin and the absence of God. They bring us close to God, but they can also estrange us from him. There is a presence of Christ in our sister or brother, but there is also selfishness and sin there; and these can even predominate. There are signs of the action of God in history, but there are also signs of the action of evil, violence, and injustice. And they too can seem to prevail.

Hence it is that mere reality, activity, commitment—even mission—are *of themselves* not sufficient basis for a spirituality or for growth in faith. Faith, hope, and love require a purer, more substantial nourishment, one without taint and admixture. This is true even in regard to the experience of God. Thus it comes about that prayer and the celebration of faith continue to be a necessary, privileged part of the way of Christian contemplation. And so it is in the word and the sacraments—the church guarantees it—that the salvific presence of God is full.

Finally, the sixth Beatitude, both as call and as promise of the vision of God, demonstrates that *men and women are made to "see God."* They are "programmed" for contemplation, as they are programmed to speak a language. We have the roots of contemplation within us, and they may not be pulled up or otherwise frustrated except under pain of dehumanization—the mutilation of our human fulfillment.

The call to the contemplation of God is universal. It is offered to everyone, but especially to the simple and the pure of heart. This is one of the teachings in the Johannine account of Jesus' meeting with the Samaritan at Jacob's well (Jn. 4:1–42). The dialogue between the Lord and this anonymous woman of the people, who has had five husbands, who shares the popular piety of her locale, and whose life is spent amid the humdrum tasks of a woman of her time, issues in Jesus' free and gratuitous revelation. " 'I know that Messiah—that is, Christ—is coming; and when he comes he will tell us everything.' 'I who am speaking to you,' said Jesus, 'I am he' " (vss. 25–26). The "living water" that Jesus offers her, after which she would "never be thirsty again" because it would "turn into a spring inside [her], welling up to eternal life" (vss. 10, 14) is actually a gift that "God is offering" (vs. 10), the grace of experiential encounter with Jesus, a grace that is here bestowed upon a simple woman of the people.

The account is paradigmatic and normative. The gift that "God is offering" is offered to everyone, even the "marginalized," the uneducated, and those who lead a hard life of daily toil. We are every one of us that Samaritan, "programmed" for the experience of God, who offers himself to us as he did to her, at all the "Jacob's wells" along the road of our life.

Mission and the Experience of God

The contemplation of God on earth, to which we are called by the sixth Beatitude, is the "living water" that roots, fertilizes, and nourishes the quality of evangelization and its fidelity to its commitment. Authentic Christian evangelizers are contemplatives. They transmit to others their own experience of God and God's kingdom. "Something . . . that we have heard, and we have seen with our own eyes; that we have watched and touched with our hands; the Word, who is life—this is our subject" (1 Jn. 1:1).

Let us specify rather more closely this profound relationship obtaining between Christian evangelization and prayer as the experience of God.

Prayer—Christian contemplation—keeps us in living contact with evangelization's most dynamic and authentic motivation. The deepest motives of mission are given to us not through pure analysis, or in simple involvement with reality, or by experience alone. The nature and specificity of evangelization are communicated to us by Christ's revelation. We know what mission is by observing the mission of Christ. We grasp evangelization when we grasp Jesus' message of the Beatitudes.

In the last analysis, the motives and basis of mission proceed from the evangelizer's faith. But faith is not a set of abstract ideas. Faith is an experience. The gospel values that motivate mission must be "experimental." That is, they must be interiorized. They must be a part of life. This requires prayer. Christian prayer in any of its forms is the only place where faith becomes an experience of Christ, his message, and his kingdom. As we have seen, without prayer the Christian experience is eviscerated and cut in half—along with the motives and deeper meaning of evangelization.

In order to be Christian, mission must provoke a very particular encounter: an experience of the presence of God and his kingdom. Again, this is something we have already observed. But we have also observed that, in order for our service and commitment to our brother and sister to be a Christian experience, an experience of the God of Jesus, we must already have had this encounter ourselves. We must already have had a living, personal experience of this God. But such encounter, and such experience, will only be the fruit of Christian prayer. God cannot be met on the road of evangelization unless we have already met him on the road of prayer. Mission rediscovers, in a new way, the presence of the Jesus we have already discovered and experienced in prayer.

Christian prayer incorporates us into the prayer of Christ the Redeemer and thereby enables us to strike a blow at the root of evil. For we share in that Redeemer's "radical evangelization." By "radical evangelization" we mean the redemption of Jesus, which strikes at the very root of our selfishness and injustice. The spring and source of these is the sin at work in the depth of the human heart and human societies. Jesus inaugurated the kingdom of God, freeing humanity from all bondage, not only by his activity and his message, but also, and more decisively, by his prayer—that prayer of his which culminated in the sacrifice of the cross. Christ's prayer and cross go further than his deeds. They are grafted onto the very root of evil, and poison that root. This is why we call Jesus' evangelization "radical," for this is what makes that evangelization absolutely and utterly decisive.

The missionary's prayer incorporates her or him into this radical evangelization of Jesus. It carries mission out beyond its own means of activity and transforms it into redemption. Evangelization is not enough, if by evangelization we merely mean activity. Mere activity is incapable of touching the crucial realities of Christian liberation. It is incapable of influencing human beings' free will, and thereby obtaining their conversion from selfishness and sin. It is incapable of any influence on the sin that lurks in the depths of human beings or their society.

Activity alone is inadequate for evangelization. Only Jesus' prayer and cross can convert the human will without doing it violence, can transform evil at its very root. Evangelization is the activity of Christ through his church, and prayer is an indispensable part of Christ's mission; hence prayer is an indispensable part of evangelization. The missionary's own prayer, then—like his or her cross—is an essential part of the mission of the church. It is the way by which we enter into collaboration with Christ, who converts free wills without forcing them and transforms selfishness at its very roots.

In mission, action and prayer form a single, coherent whole. Missionary activity cannot replace the effectiveness of prayer; but neither can prayer replace missionary activity. We may not entrust to prayer what should be a matter of effort and human intelligence, a matter of what God expects from the faculties he himself has bestowed on human beings.

Prayer accompanies the activity of evangelization and invests it with lucidity, constancy, and steadfastness. But it does not replace it. Its efficacy is, rather, on the level of the "radical evangelization" of which we have just spoken—the conversion and redemption of human beings, together with the real world about them, right in the roots of their slavery and selfishness.

Prayer, as experience of God and as participation in redemption (the two inseparable aspects of "contemplation in action"), *generates a particular missionary style and spirituality in the evangelizer,* a style proper to Christian evangelization. Accordingly it requires of the evangelizer a lifestyle in harmony with this spirituality.

Prayer calls for a "pure heart" in the sense of the sixth Beatitude. It demands that we neither worship idols in our heart nor go in pursuit of them in our acts. Thus a lifestyle is implied that will integrate the requirements of mission with those of contemplation, a lifestyle that will enable us to "see God" in prayer and evangelization alike.

Faced with these exigencies, a missionary lifestyle will have to respond by allowing real "space for God." The missionary will have to have a capacity for reflection, for interiorization, for "being still" in his or her inmost depths. A certain personal discipline will be required, a certain self-control in the area of sense and affectivity. We shall have to "stay in charge" of our own activity, which has a tendency to pull us along instead, sometimes to the point of enslaving us. Even our work, our activity can transform itself into an idol and corrupt the evangelical quality of mission.

"Pure heart, clean hands." This is the formula of the sixth Beatitude for a lifestyle that will make it possible for mission and the experience of God to walk hand in hand, to their mutual enhancement.

The synthesis of mission and contemplation is a constantly recurring biblical theme, in the Old Testament as in the New. The Bible portrays for us the ideal missionary contemplative in its picture of the prophets. From Moses to Christ—in Elijah, for instance, John the Baptist, or the prophets of the exile—the biblical prophet is the emissary of God charged with the task of calling the people to follow the one, true, unmanipulable God, ever denouncing their new idolatries. At the same time a prophet is a disciple, whose own heart God has purified, and to whom he has revealed himself in a religious experience that can be startlingly dramatic.

In biblical symbology the prophet is sent by turns to the "city," to evangelize, and to the "desert," to deepen his experience of God. Moses, Elijah, other Old Testament prophets, John the Baptist, even Jesus, prepare for their mission in the desert and return there at certain moments in their lives. The biblical "desert" is more than a place. It is a biblical symbol. On the one hand, the desert is a place of solitude and poverty, where the heart is purified, idols are unmasked, and God is experienced intensely and exclusively. It is the place of Christian contemplation. On the other hand, the desert is a symbol of the sterility and rock-hard soil of the human heart, which the prophet is sent to convert. John the Baptist "preached in the wilderness" (Mt. 3:1). That is, he evangelized the desert of a sinful society.

The biblical prophets are the prototypes of the Christian evangelizer. The alternation in their lives of mission to the city and experience of God in the desert is a symbol of the twofold task to be realized in the human heart. As such they are but the two dimensions of one and the same prophetic mission.

Every evangelizer is called upon to make this synthesis. Every evangelizer is called to join the courage of a prophet's commitment to a contemplative's experience of God.

9

THE GOSPEL OF TRUE PEACE

Happy the peacemakers:
they shall be called sons of God [Mt. 5:9].

The seventh Beatitude is not concerned merely with being "peaceful"—with simply doing what lies within us in order to be at peace with others. It is concerned with *making* peace. It is addressed to those who actively and positively commit themselves to making a contribution, in the concrete circumstances of their real lives, work, and whatever influence they may have in the world, to the upbuilding of peace.

To "work for peace" is to foster the rapprochement, the reconciliation, and thereby also the brotherly and sisterly communion of persons, families, and social groups that are divided or engaged in conflict with one another. This disposition is set forth as a Beatitude, for it is a participation in the attitude of Christ the Happy One, and Christ the Evangelizer, whose mission is aptly described in the Bible as that of the restoration of human beings' peace, of their permanent reconciliation with God and with one another after the "scattering" and division inflicted upon them by sin, hatred, and injustice (cf. Jn. 11:52).

Isaiah refers to the Christ to come as the "Prince of Peace" (Isa. 9:5) and the mighty deed of his kingdom as the actualization of true peace among all men and women:

> Wide is his dominion
> in a peace that has no end, . . .
> . . . these will hammer their swords into plowshares,
> their spears into sickles.
> Nation will not lift sword against nation,
> there will be no more training for war. . . .
> The wolf lives with the lamb,
> the panther lies down with the kid . . . [Isa. 9:6; 2:4; 11:6].

In the biblical view, the coming of peace among human beings is possible only to the extent that human beings are reconciled with God, only in the measure that they return to communion with him. Being at peace with God is the evangelical condition for the promotion of peace among human beings. To evangelize is "to proclaim the Lord's year of favor" (Lk. 4:19; cf. Isa. 61:2), and the evangelizer is the messenger who proclaims peace (cf. Rom. 10:15). Peace is the gift of Christ, who made himself the victim of our reconciliation:

> Peace I bequeath to you,
> my own peace I give you,
> a peace the world cannot give. . . .
> Peace be with you . . . [Jn. 14:27; 20:19].

> For he is the peace between us, and has made the two into one and broken down the barrier which used to keep them apart, actually destroying in his own person the hostility . . . restoring peace through the cross, to unite them both in a single Body and reconcile them with God [Eph. 2:14-16].

In a word, to work for peace means to evangelize. It means consolidating the communion of women and men with God and one another.

How is one to work for true peace—the peace that is the fruit of the gospel of God? How may one hope to escape a deceptive peace, a "peace" based on fear, force, and the institutionalization of division and injustice? The basic principle of the answer to this question is given to us in one of the preceding Beatitudes, which lays the groundwork for a Christian understanding of peace.

Mercy moves us to deeds of solidarity with our sisters and brothers in need. It inspires us to deliver them from their miseries, and thereby to reestablish justice. Mercy moves us to forgive their offenses and be reconciled with them. In the perspective of evangelization according to the Beatitudes, peace is the work of justice and of forgiveness, both of which are inseparable from the law of mercy.

In a previous chapter we reflected on mercy as active involvement with our brother and sister. We noted that it creates an actual communion with these brothers and sisters. Now let us reflect on forgiveness and reconciliation, the second of the twin paths of communion and peace.

In the Service of Reconciliation

Evangelization can be defined in terms of liberation for communion, or it can be defined in terms of reconciliation. From the point of view of mission and its spirituality, liberation and reconciliation are complementary. Concretely they are both constitutive of a Christian community of sisters and brothers. Evangelization according to the spirit of the Beatitudes is a ministry of reconciliation for communion and peace.

What precisely is reconciliation? Reconciliation is a return to friendship—to the condition of brothers and sisters—among persons, families, social groups, or nations, which, instead of responding to the call to communion, have burst the bonds of that friendship, or that condition of brothers and sisters. Reconciliation, then, is more than "conciliation"—which is a relatively provisional agreement of some kind. Reconciliation is the restoration of communion destroyed. This is why reconciliation always carries the connotation of return, reconstruction, reencounter.

Obviously the notion of reconciliation is not a specifically and exclusively Christian one. True, it is a marvelously apt characterization of the work of Christ who came to reconcile human beings with God and with one another. But the notion of reconciliation also has validity in the area of human relations in general, including, of course, social and political ones. Politicians speak of "national reconciliation," or of reconciliation after a conflict or confrontation between nations. Clearly the notion of reconciliation corresponds to a human ideal, a law of society. The history of societies and peoples is shot through with a dialectic of conflict, of injustices perpetrated by human beings on one another, and at the same time their efforts to reestablish peace, understanding, and reconciliation.

But the discourse of reconciliation is too often inadequate. Frequently it is the tool of particular ideological interests in the attainment of their political ends. "Reconciliation" can even be proposed as a substitute for the resolution of legitimate conflict. Reconciliation is not something to be used as a cloak for social abuses, crimes, and sin.

Hence we must situate reconciliation in an evangelical perspective, and proclaim it, with all that it requires and demands, as a part of mission. The demands of Christian reconciliation are the demands of peace, and peace may be defined as consolidated reconciliation, in the form of *justice* and *pardon*.

The reestablishment of justice is a condition for Christian reconciliation. It is not hard to see that the most frequent causes of division and deterioration in the relationships of groups or peoples who are called, by reason of their history, geography, or human ties, to live as sisters and brothers are certain injustices— various forms of abuse and exploitation of human being by human being. In conditions of ongoing, unresolved injustice, a simple proposal of reconciliation is unrealistic. Except in cases of great evangelical maturity, to call for reconciliation within an actual, ongoing context of injustice is simply asking too much of human psychology. Hence the church, in a biblical tradition stemming from the prophet Isaiah, teaches that the reconciliation that leads to true peace must be the work of justice (cf. *Gaudium et Spes*, no. 78; *Pacem in Terris*, no. 167; *Populorum Progressio*, no. 76; Medellín, *Document on Peace*, no. 14).

Justice on the march clears roadblocks. It removes the obstacles presented by conflicts and resentments that have been provoked by past injustices and abuses and thereby opens the way for reconciliation. But this is only trail-blazing. Of itself such preparatory activity is insufficient to constitute reconciliation. Even a just accord and the abolition of all injustices to the satisfaction of both parties are not enough to re-create a community of brothers and sisters. Such community transcends simple "justice." Such community presupposes the reestablishment of encounter. It requires forms of actual communion. It is possible to live in "justice" and nevertheless live isolated and withdrawn. A community can be practicing "justice"—no one has any complaints against anyone else—and not be practicing love and mercy. There is a kind of "justice" that is very cold indeed.

The reason for this is that the simple implementation of justice, upon the satisfactory resolution of conflict, has no power to heal old wounds and wipe out past offenses. In the course of any hostile human confrontation, the parties do actual injury to each other. The memory and consequences of these objective offenses perdure, beyond the termination of the conflict and the restoration of external justice. Resentment continues to rankle in the hearts of the offended on both sides, preventing them from consummating the process of their reconciliation in the reestablishment of lost friendship or communion.

Hence something else is required for reconciliation and the consolidation of peace: the forgiveness of one another's offenses. This is true for individuals, families, social groups, and nations alike. Only forgiveness can efface the vestiges of conflict and open free passage to reconciliation. One of the uses of that mercy which transcends human justice and the liberation it bears humankind is pardon.

In the New Testament, too, reconciliation and peace are the effects of pardon and forgiveness. This doctrine is wonderfully synthesized in the Beatitudes of mercy and of peacemaking. Here, as Jesus completes and perfects the old law, the demands that these two dynamisms make on human beings are incorporated into the Christian message itself:

You have learned how it was said: *You must love your neighbor* and hate your enemy. But I say this to you: love your enemies and pray for those who persecute you; in this way you will be sons of your Father in heaven, for he causes his sun to rise on bad men as well as good, and his rain to fall

on honest and dishonest men alike. For if you love those who
love you, what right have you to claim any credit? [Mt.
5:43–46].

In concrete, actual practice, to love one's enemy will mean to
forgive from the heart and to be entirely ready actually to be
reconciled at the appropriate moment.

The necessity of forgiveness for the re-creation of any human
community of understanding is not an exigency only of Christianity and its spirituality; even in political life men and women
are aware of this need. They know that, without an effort to
forget the offenses of the past and to staunch its wounds, "national reconciliation" after conflict is very difficult indeed. This
is why amnesties are granted. Amnesty is the secular, political
correlate of forgiveness. Amnesty following conflict is not of
itself reconciliation; but it creates the necessary political conditions for a "new start." It creates an atmosphere of reconciliation. It creates the possibility of forgiveness. When amnesty is
offered (on both sides of the conflict) on a basis of genuine justice, it is an effective means and aid to reconciliation within
human groups.

*Nevertheless we have always to remind ourselves that reconcil-
iation is an exigency that ought actually to accompany the
process of conflict from the very outset.* Reconciliation is not
something we "come up with" after the hostilities are all over,
after enmity has subsided and a satisfactory accord has been
reached. We dare not lose sight of the actual goal of community
and social relationships at all levels, even in the processes of
struggle and conflict themselves. This goal is the reconciliation
of individuals and social groups. If this goal is not kept in view
from the very beginning, forgiveness and reconciliation will be
found to be extremely difficult at the end. Even during the
course of conflict, then, the notion of a call to reconciliation is
to be kept alive, lest it be frustrated in the event. Thus the demand for reconciliation fulfills its role of humanizing conflicts
from the very start of those conflicts.

Conflicts, social struggle, even war can be processes either of
humanization or of dehumanization. Even confrontations are
subject to ethics. The ethics of conflict will consist, in large

measure, of respect for human rights, especially on the part of the parties to the conflict. Regard for human rights by both sides of a conflict can actually humanize the conflict. The violation of human rights, on the other hand, dehumanizes conflicts, provoking unnecessary wounds and offenses, which ultimately cause grave difficulties. For when the moment of reconciliation arrives, the memory of the human rights violations abides.

When we say that the mystique of reconciliation must accompany human conflict from the beginning, we do not mean merely that it must be present as an aspiration—actually to be promoted only when the confrontation finally subsides; we mean that it must be actually operative, that it must be at work creating a humanizing attitude during the whole conflictive process. The vitality of a spirituality of reconciliation is verified in its special emphasis on respect for ethics and human rights in times of confrontation. Such respect will do much to facilitate amnesty, forgiveness, and reconciliation when the proper moment arrives. It will have created, in advance, the interior dispositions corresponding to these functions of mercy. Atrocities, cruelty, acts of revenge, every form of violation of human rights in the course of conflict sunder and demolish the condition of brothers and sisters; and when the moment has come to rebuild this condition, the required spiritual attitude will be lacking, and factually impossible to exact of all parties. Now it will require one or two generations to reestablish the conditions of equanimity that make reconciliation possible.

Evangelization is the simultaneous proclamation of a liberating justice and of reconciliation. It is identification with the poor and oppressed and it is forgiveness of our neighbor's offenses simultaneously. No human communion can be created in the absence of either of these two conditions. To evangelize in the spirit of the Beatitudes means following Christ, the Merciful Liberator. Evangelization is the act whereby we convey to his disciples both of these attitudes—and thereby construct a Christian community of sisters and brothers upon a basis of justice and reconciliation.

A synthesis of these demands at the heart of reality is surely no easy matter. It requires a mature spirituality in the evangelizer, and wisdom and sound pedagogy in the practice of evangelization. One must voyage precariously between the Scylla of division and resentment and the Charybdis of pseudo-unity and resigned conformism. Reconciliation is not a luxury. Without it, liberation cannot be humanizing, nor will it be able to prevent the recurrence of the erstwhile condition of oppression and injustice. For reconciliation to be viable and lasting, justice must prevail.

In concrete practice, the evangelizer must be able to discern the proper "pedagogical moment." He or she must know when to emphasize the struggle for justice and when to emphasize forgiveness and reconciliation. Of course neither will be promoted to the exclusion of the other. The "discernment" in question is a matter of emphasis in function of opportunities presented. In some situations a call for reconciliation will have the ring of a prophetic denunciation of injustice; in others, it will sound altogether like an attempt to legitimize these injustices. What the gospel asks is that we maintain the synthesis of the demands of justice and reconciliation inherent in the Beatitude of mercy, and thus conquer the temptation of systematic one-sidedness in the application of this Beatitude to real life.

Ultimately this application is a matter of the rebuilding of Christian community. After all, a communion of brothers and sisters is the only true sign of genuine peace. And to evangelize means to work for peace.

10

ASCENDING THE MOUNT OF MARTYRDOM

Happy those who are persecuted in the cause of right:
theirs is the kingdom of heaven.

Happy are you when people abuse you and persecute you and
speak all kinds of calumny against you on my account. Re-
joice and be glad, for your reward will be great in heaven . . .
                                                    [Mt. 5:10–12].

The last Beatitude in Luke and the last Beatitude in Matthew
coincide. For both evangelists—the one who tells us who is
happy and the one who tells us how to be happy, the one who
expounds the criteria for mission and the one who presents the
spirituality of the missioner—the following of Christ the
Evangelizer is crowned with persecution. Persecution is at once
the ultimate criterion of mission and the ultimate quality of the
spirituality of the missioner. The road of the Beatitudes has led
us to the highest degree of identification with Jesus: persecution
and martyrdom.

There are other characteristics, besides their mutual convergence, that distinguish the last Matthean and Lucan Beatitudes from all the others in each series. First, unlike the first
three Beatitudes in Luke, the fourth is not pronounced upon any
particular category of persons. Similarly, unlike its seven prede-
cessors in Matthew, the eighth Beatitude does not proclaim a

habitual attitude to be acquired. Jesus is speaking to us here of an eventuality. No one is permanently persecuted or martyred. Persecution is something that comes unexpectedly—although, of course, once unleashed, it may continue without let-up. But when it comes, momentary or prolonged, late or soon, Jesus enjoins us to receive it as a "beatitude"—at once a grace and a demand, foreseen by him for us and pertaining to his true discipleship.

Second, the promise that Jesus joins to this Beatitude is a special one. All the Beatitudes promise the kingdom of God; but here the evangelists promise it with the enthusiasm and vigor of a reward altogether special, a peerless crown of glory. For once, they depart from the austere language of the other Beatitudes in order to emphasize the special significance and extraordinary grace offered here in the last: "Rejoice when that day comes and dance for joy, for then your reward will be great in heaven" (Lk. 6:23).

The last Beatitude, then has a special eschatological paschal value. It points more explicitly to the resurrection, the sequel to the cross. For "if we are children we are heirs as well: heirs of God and coheirs with Christ, sharing his sufferings so as to share his glory" (Rom. 8:17). After all, Jesus has told us:

> Unless a wheat grain falls on the ground and dies,
> it remains only a single grain;
> but if it dies,
> it yields a rich harvest.
> Anyone who loves his life loses it;
> anyone who hates his life in this world
> will keep it for the eternal life [Jn. 12:24–25].

Ultimately, then, the last Beatitude is the Beatitude of the Christian cross.

Let us specify more closely the meaning of this Beatitude. We are dealing with persecution here in the broad sense of the word: ". . . hate you, drive you out, abuse you, denounce your name as criminal" (Lk. 6:22); ". . . abuse you and persecute you and speak all kinds of calumny against you" (Mt. 5:11). Not only physical persecution is meant, and not only psychological violence, but every form of hostility, pressure (sometimes subtle), harassment, mistrust, and misunderstanding arising from the fact of being a disciple of Jesus. In this sense persecution is a "relative eventuality"—however certain a one—in the Christian life. For the missionary, however, it is an essential part of his or her commitment. For "there is no one who has left house, brothers, sisters, father, children or land for my sake and for the sake of the gospel who will not be repaid a hundred times over . . .—not without persecutions—now in this present time and in the world to come, eternal life" (Mk. 10:30).

There are many degrees of persecution, both in intensity and in duration. When it is to the death, persecution is called martyrdom. Martyrdom is the supreme degree of the last Beatitude. Here identification with Christ persecuted, judged, and executed achieves its plenitude. This is why the church canonizes martyrs without further question, without any official inquiry into their past life.

Persecution is "happy" when it is "in the cause of right"; that is, when it is in the cause of the justice of the kingdom, that justice which is the sum and substance of all the values and truths Jesus has brought us. Not every persecution is a "happy" one, for not every cause is a happy one. The cause must be right and just.

But from this it follows that the disciples of Jesus will be "happy" not only when they suffer for the faith, or for explicitly religious values, but also when, inspired by the gospel, they embrace the cause of human justice, the cause of the weak, the cause of human rights—the cause of truth. What qualifies them as persecuted "on account of the Son of Man" (Lk. 6:22) is the evangelical basis of their commitment and the authenticity of the human and Christian value to which they are dedicated, to the point of having to suffer for it.

As with all the Beatitudes, Jesus is also the unique model of the last Beatitude. He is the paradigm and norm of the one persecuted in the cause of justice and right, even to death on a cross. Being persecuted in the cause of right has the status of a Beatitude only because Jesus was rejected, insulted, calumniated, and sacrificed. He is the very incarnation of this Beatitude, just as he is of all the others. He teaches us what persecution and cross mean when it come to evangelization and human liberation. He teaches us how to accept persecution—both how to react externally and what attitude to take in the hour of persecution.

Jesus is the sole, the perfect Happy One, and we participate in his lot only in a relative, imperfect way. For only Jesus' persecution and martyrdom have been "full testimony." After all, only Jesus was absolutely just, and only his persecution absolutely unjust. We are not that just. In us there is always error, vacillation, and fault. Hence also the persecution of the disciple is never altogether and absolutely unjust.

This is a fact it will behoove us to recall whenever we are tempted to take pride in the face of persecution in any of its various forms. It will help us vanquish the easy temptation to deem ourselves victims and martyrs. The badge of this Beatitude is the "humility of the persecuted," the consciousness of our own possible errors and faults—notwithstanding which , however, we share in the grace and promise of this Beatitude.

It is not to be wondered at, then, if the story of the persecuted Christians and their martyrs—including those of Latin America in our day—is never without some taint, some adulteration or admixture in the purity of their motivation, just as the motives of the persecutors are never absolutely and utterly evil. Not everything is always purely "for God and the faith." There are political and ideological elements present. There may have been imprudences and errors on the part of these martyrs. The Roman Emperors had good reasons of state for persecuting Christians; the same is often true under totalitarian governments today (although here the case is rather more subtle). This in no way divests persecution of its abusive, unjust character, nor does it deprive the victim of persecution in the cause of right of his or her Beatitude. It is only that the victim does have faults. He or she is guilty of some imprudence. In view of this it is always necessary to consider each case individually—no easy matter during the actual course of events, events charged with emotions, mixed motives, and ideological interests. In order to discern the authentic martyr or victim of persecution in the cause of right, an outlook and an equanimity are required, which can only come with a certain distance and passing of time.

Finally, the Beatitude of persecution "closes the book," sets a seal on the message of evangelization in Luke and Matthew. For, as it constitutes the ultimate identification with Jesus, it puts a price on the other Beatitudes: the various kinds of persecution are what await disciples who evangelize, when they have taken seriously the criteria that Jesus the Happy One calls upon them to embrace. The last Beatitude is the proof of Christ's fidelity to the mission entrusted to him by the Father. It is likewise proof of our own fidelity to mission in the spirit of the Beatitudes.

If you make an option for the poor, if you call in question the wealth of the rich and the power of the mighty, if you question all the false felicities, if you practice radical poverty of heart, if you are on fire for the justice of the kingdom, if your mercy refuses to discriminate and your pardon and reconciliation know no bounds, if you struggle with idols within and without, and if you respond to all the other demands of Luke and Matthew for following Jesus—sooner or later you will pay the price. And the price is persecution, all manner of persecution, which the disciple of Jesus must undergo to whatever extent his or her commitments and involvements go contrary to the interests of human beings and their unjust, sinful society.

The Missionary Meaning of the Cross

The Beatitude of the persecutions is the Beatitude of the various forms of the cross in evangelization. It is not merely the Beatitude of the great cross of martyrdom. It is the Beatitude of all the crosses of Christian commitment.

The cross of Jesus is the sign of the steadfastness of his love for the kingdom of God. We must not separate Jesus' death from the rest of his life. Jesus' martyrdom is the catastrophic outcome of all his words and works. And it is a logical outcome, one altogether consonant with the course of those words and works. The cross is the symbol of his utter loyalty to his Father. It cannot be separated from the persecutions and conflicts that preceded it, nor from Jesus' criteria, options, and attitudes, nor from his preaching. By his revelation of the one true God, by his challenge to the religious decadence of his time and its distortions of that God, by his solicitude and predilection for sinners and the poor, by the combat he waged against the idols of his society, and by his questioning of the false values of that society—Jesus himself unintentionally unleashed the storm that carried him to the cross.

The predictable consequence of following Jesus the Evangelizer is suffering. A certain type of Christian piety is inclined to separate Jesus' cross from the events of his life that preceded it. Devotion to the cross, so characteristic of the Latin American people, is in itself a precious thing. But frequently it is the veneration of too solitary a cross. This veneration honors the passion and death of our Lord in isolation—in isolation not only from what was to come (the resurrection), but from what had gone before: the manner and content of the gospel message, which of course is what actually brought Jesus to that cross. The cross is not an isolated, arbitrary element in the Father's design. It is the "period" at the end of a life of absolute dedication to the cause of the kingdom, and Jesus accepted it with all his love. The passion of Christ not only expresses the love and loyalty Jesus experienced at that particular moment; it expresses his fidelity to the kingdom throughout all the persecutions that had gone before and that paved the way for the denouement of the cross.

In the spirituality of the missionary, the various forms in which cross and persecution present themselves along the road of a life of fidelity to the justice of the kingdom—including perhaps even martyrdom—are part and parcel of mission itself. They are the proof that this missioner's evangelization is Christian. They are the sign of mission's persevering efficacy. Ever disconcerting, ever enveloped in the clouds of faith, persecutions are the special signs of authentic evangelization.

Jesus underwent a persecution to the death. This tremendous event is a revelation of the power of evil, of sin and selfishness with all their consequences, with all the determination of their opposition to the kingdom of God.

Throughout his mission, from its very outset, Jesus experienced evil as a positive and powerful reality—the "hour of darkness," he called it. The power of evil in Jesus' mission is not to be underestimated. He found it expressed in the sins and injustices that were typical of the people of the society of his time, just as we find it expressed in the sins and injustices that are typical of our time. Indeed, evil not only brought Jesus to his death—his life's apparent failure—it also frustrated his immediate design for the propagation of the kingdom, which would be the conversion of Israel and popular acceptance of his work. This meant the apparent failure of his mission as well. Jesus crucified is a convincing demonstration of the power and persistence of evil.

The negative lesson of the cross is that evil is pervasive in history, that it will appear in ever new guises, that its stubborn persistence is a tragic fact of reality, that its opposition to the values of the kingdom of God is constant, and that, today as ever, it is capable of carrying the work of the church, together with the missionary effort of each of us, in any given instance (although not everywhere and always), down the road of failure.

The cross teaches us that evangelization has a profound dimension of struggle against evil and sin, as concretely expressed today in the arms race, disrespect for life, the corruption of love, the exploitation of human beings by human beings, hunger, misery, materialism, and all manner of injustice. Evil is mighty, perduring, collective, and recurring. It can throttle evangelization. It can bring the cause of the kingdom to its apparent failure.

At times, in judging the influence of the church and the influence of Christianity and struck with the tenuousness of their effect for good, we have a tendency to think that this fragility is due to the church's lack of credibility with those it evangelizes, stemming in turn from a failure to update its forms of evangelization. There may be some truth here. But it is also true that, once upon a dark moment in history, the power of evil dashed to the earth the earthly work of Christ himself, whose credibility and genuineness were total. That power of evil should surely find it no more difficult to paralyze and destroy the work of our evangelization. The reality of the cross, powerful proof of the existence of evil, places us on our guard against any sanguine overoptimism in its regard.

But the paradox of the cross consists in this: in spite of its mighty message about the power of evil and sin, it is its message of hope that prevails. Despite the presence of evil, the cross triumphs over it most decisively, to become the sign of our sure hope in mission—in its effectiveness and in its ultimate and definitive victory over every form of sin.

This is the paradox of the cross, that at first it seems a failure for it is the death of Jesus, the failure of the cause of the kingdom, and the persecution and collapse of evangelization. And yet, because of this same Jesus, who passed from death to life, transforming the cross into a source of new life and total liberation, that cross also constitutes the irreversible commencement of evil's radical annihilation. As we have said when we were speaking of prayer: evil, in order to be overcome, needs redemption. Persecution and the cross are the redemptive dimension of mission. Where human means are powerless to strike at the root of all evils and all injustices, all suffering, and all the crosses that come with evangelizing, the cross incorporates us into the persecution and martyrdom of Christ; whereupon, being grafted along with him onto the root of evil, we now cooperate with him in its definitive dissolution, to become liberators and redeemers ourselves. Thus in marvelous wise do we "make up all that has still to be undergone by Christ for the sake of his body, the Church" (Col. 1:24).

The cross is the sign of Christian hope. It teaches us that evil, selfishness, and injustice do not have the last word in history. History's last word is the word of right, of justice, of peace, of a communion of sisters and brothers.

The concrete course of history shows us both realities intertwined: evil and good, injustice and justice, sin and grace. In the very midst of the burgeoning kingdom of God in all its manifestations, evil perdures. But the reality of the cross is the foundation for a radical optimism with respect to mission—not only because the kingdom we so arduously and painfully anticipate today is destined to be the last and sole reality of the future, but also because we know that this perduring evil can itself be converted into good, even in the course of history. Because of the cross, evil is transformed into a wellspring of higher good. For "we know that by turning everything to their good God cooperates with all those who love him" (Rom. 8:28), as Paul said, and the reason why is that, in Jesus, the evil of the cross became the grace of total liberation.

Ultimately only the cross is of any use in comprehending the mystery of evil. Surely this is a mystery that is insoluble apart from the Christian perspective. Only the cross reveals the deep, original identity of evangelization, where evil constitutes the missionary's great temptation. Jesus himself has put us on our guard against the temptation of acedia, of discouragement in the face of the persistence of evil, of impatience with the unremitting confrontation between good and evil, between the gospel and sin, at every turn—coupled with the difficulty of distinguishing the one from the other! "Lord," we are tempted to cry out, with the field hands in the parable of the Darnel, "do you want us to go and weed it out," try to distinguish the evil from the good and do away with it altogether?

But he said, "No, because when you weed out the darnel you might pull up the wheat with it. Let them both grow till the harvest; and at harvest time I shall say to the reapers: First collect the darnel and tie it in bundles to be burned, then gather the wheat into my barn" [Mt. 13:28–30].

Only after Jesus had submitted to the cross and been raised again did the disciples discover the key with which to decipher this parable in all its meaning for mission.

Redeemers with Jesus

The Beatitude of persecution reveals the conflictual nature of evangelization. In its character as confrontation between the justice of the kingdom and the tendencies of selfishness, sin, and error, mission is conflictual of its very nature. It necessarily causes suffering. It is the cross. Nowhere in the message of Jesus do we hear that we are to live without conflict. Quite the contrary, contradiction and the cross are among Jesus' most insistently repeated prophecies to his disciples. But he has taught us how to react to it. He has taught us how to be faithful to mission in the midst of conflict. He has likewise taught us the redemptive meaning of these conflicts. More than by his words, it is by the example of his life—by his manner of furthering the cause of the kingdom—that Jesus is our Way through the midst of the conflicts of evangelization.

There is no question here of literal, historical imitation of Jesus' missionary journey. No one is expected to reproduce the particular conflicts Jesus encountered on his own path. Entirely apart from the fact that every missionary process is unique, and that the historical and religious conditions in which Jesus acted were very different from ours today, the mission of Jesus was also unique in itself. Jesus is the Son of God, the Redeemer, and his path and purposes incalculably surpass any missionary endeavor of later ages. We as evangelizers can but participate in the redemptive and liberating deed of Jesus and draw from it the inspiration for our own commitment. Ours is a process of permitting ourselves to be evangelized along the conflictual path of mission. Jesus has taken our experiences upon himself in advance and has taught us the correct attitude to have in our efforts to bear up under them. Jesus the Evangelizer knew persecution, success, failure, disappointment, joy, anticipation, the need to change his missionary strategy in mid-course, loneliness, misunderstanding, and martyrdom. As evangelizers ourselves, we discover a wellspring of spirituality in these experiences of his. Now Jesus' experiences become our own.

What especially interests us here is Jesus' internal conflicts, in their function as light and grace for the evangelization of our own experience. The outward chronicle of Jesus' persecutions and conflicts is familiar. Jesus fought a running battle with the religious leaders of Israel, and the hostilities culminated in persecution and execution. With few exceptions, Jesus encountered only hostility and mistrust on the part of the Roman political and military power, the ruling class. He was constantly calumniated. Whatever he said was distorted. His disciples misunderstood him, and in the moment of crisis they abandoned him.

So much for the outward facts. Now let us attempt to penetrate the interior suffering of this Son of God, together with the steadfastness and love with which he accepted it. For it is the interior life of Christ the Evangelizer, the One persecuted in the cause of the kingdom, which, more than the outward contingencies of his life, becomes for us the spring and source of a missionary mystique.

Let us consider two phenomena that lie at the root of Christ's interior suffering that will also be the cause of trial and suffering in the mission of the church. They are temptation, and loneliness, or isolation.

Jesus was tempted. Not apparently tempted, but really tempted. Nor was such a circumstance incompatible with his divinity, which had taken on the human condition "in all things save sin." Temptation is not sin. It is not even imperfection. It is enticement. Jesus' temptations were temptations and nothing more. He resisted them utterly. With us, things are different. Our resistance to temptation is not so absolute as his. At times our temptation actually crosses over into the area of the sinful.

Jesus' temptations make their appearance from the first moment of his missionary activity. In his forty days in the desert, before he undertook his missionary activity, Jesus had to undergo temptation at the hands of the devil (Mt. 4:1-11; Mk. 1:12-13; Lk. 4:1-13). The three temptations on the Mount of the Fast are the paradigm of all Jesus' temptations. Their narrative form is that of a parable, but their content reveals to us the nature of the basic temptation of Christ.

From the particular viewpoint of evangelization—which, of course, does not exhaust the meaning and message of the temptations of the wilderness—the three temptations recounted are essentially one and the same. Each is the same seduction on the part of evil, but presented in a different guise each time. "If you are the Son of God, tell this stone to turn into a loaf. . . . I will give you all this power and the glory of these kingdoms. . . . Worship me, then, and it shall all be yours. . . . If you are the Son of God . . . throw yourself down from here," from the parapet of the Temple, "for scripture says: He will put his angels in charge of you to guard you . . ." (Lk. 4:3-10).

All three temptations repeat the one great temptation of Jesus as the Evangelizer. But the demon's enticement is subtle. He does not attempt overtly to withdraw Jesus from his mission. He does not say to him, "You have the power of the Son of God. Divorce that power from your mission to establish the kingdom and use it for some other purpose. Use your divine condition to your own advantage." No, this would have been too crass, too obvious. The actual temptation is more subtle. And it is more dangerous. It is more difficult to recognize as a temptation. It is presented as a value. The demon merely suggests that Jesus

fulfill the mission he has received from his Father—in a new
way. He tempts Jesus to be unfaithful to the *modality* of that
mission—to the criteria, options, attitudes, and values proper to
the kingdom of God and the Beatitudes. It is as if the demon had
said to him, "Make use of your power as Son of God to work
your way into favor with the people. Fascinate them. Bewilder
them with portents. You can be a great leader! You can be the
ruler of your people if you simply establish the theocratic kingdom they want. You have prestige. Institutionalize it! What
power and glory you shall have upon earth!"

But the missionary strategy the demon proposes is incompatible with Jesus' firm, unshakable option. Jesus has received
another mandate from his Father, and he is determined to carry
it out. He has not come to set himself up as a civil ruler or social
leader or temporal liberator. He has not come to found the
kingdom by might or to institutionalize his prestige for his own
benefit and that of earthly causes. The thrust of his mission is
redemption and radical liberation. He has not come to force
himself upon consciences or to hypnotize people's minds, but
simply to offer them the Good News, without doing them any
external or interior violence, and rely on their free acceptance of
faith and conversion. His missionary path is not one of power
and prestige, but of the cross, persecution, and the spirit of the
Beatitudes.

Accordingly Jesus utterly resists and rejects the temptation of
the devil. But it will reappear. In other moments of his life Jesus
will have to face basically the same temptation. Temptation is
part of the human condition and inherent in the Christian mission. "The devil left him, to return at the appointed time," Luke
tells us ominously (Lk. 4:13) at the conclusion of his narrative.

The "appointed time" comes in other critical situations in
Jesus' mission. The wilderness temptation is to be repeated. It
will be presented in different forms. But it will always consist in
the temptation to exchange the orientation of a religious messianism proper to a prophet, proper to the "Servant of Yahweh" especially, a messianism in the service of redemption from
sin, for a "messianism" that is temporal and triumphalistic.
Often it is the people themselves who are the purveyors of this
temptation.

We find an example in one of the occasions on which the people want to make Jesus a king, a temporal messiah. Jesus had just performed the multiplication of the loaves, and those who had followed him—by the thousands—were filled with enthusiasm (Jn. 6:1-14). This was temptation for Jesus. But his resistance was radical and complete. He fled to another part of the shore (Jn. 6:15) and then confronted the people with his true messianism (Jn. 6:22-58).

The same temptation recurs at the end of Jesus' life as he entered Jerusalem for the last time. His entry was a triumphal one, and the people followed him shouting and crying out (Mt. 21:1-11). The event was an expression of religious fervor, of course. But it had political overtones. It was an invitation to Jesus to make use of his prestige of the moment on behalf of a temporal cause. Jesus refused to yield. He resisted the temptation.

But the Redeemer's mightiest and most crucial temptation is reserved for the night of his passion. On the very threshold of martyrdom, he has to face the last offensive of the tempter. It is Jesus' last opportunity to unburden himself—to divest himself of the mission of "Servant of Yahweh" and exchange the humiliations of the cross for "the power and the glory" (Lk. 4:6)—and the temptation is intensely dramatic. It comes upon Jesus like a storm, during his prayer on the Mount of Olives (Lk. 22:39-46). "Father," he prays, "if you are willing, take this cup," this temptation, "away from me. Nevertheless, let your will"—the rejection of the temptation—"be done, not mine" (Lk. 22:42). Again and again Jesus prays, "repeating the same words" (Mt. 26:44). So intense is the crisis that his "soul is sorrowful to the point of death" (Mt. 26:38; cf. Mk. 14:34), and his perspiration turns to drops of blood (Lk. 22:44). But the temptation is overcome at last, and Jesus lays down his life—the crowning act of fidelity to his mission.

Jesus' experience of temptation has much to teach us regarding the temptations we ourselves have to face in the course of our evangelizing. First, it tells us that temptations—all types of temptations—are "connatural" to mission. They are part of what we might call "interior persecution"—interior conflict. Jesus has taught us how to overcome them, not how to eliminate them.

Second, Jesus' experience teaches us that the most typical

temptation for the evangelizing church and its members will be the temptation to rely on human methods. We shall be tempted to use temporal means, "the power and the glory," instead of the gospel of the Beatitudes and the following of Jesus. Our temptation will be to substitute other "kingdoms" for the kingdom of Christ, to replace Christian evangelization with "something just as good"—that is, with a caricature of evangelization. We shall be tempted to replace the criteria, options, and demands of the kingdom with criteria, options, and demands more in keeping with a temporal enterprise. Jesus utterly rejected this temptation. But the members of his church are not Jesus. They may yield to it. Perhaps it will be only a little, and perhaps it will not be altogether consciously. They may make some slight reduction in the quality of mission, take it down a notch or so. Or they may remember the primacy of the Beatitudes in principle—but forget it in practice. These are the moments of a possible missionary, and ecclesial, decadence. It will be the task of the Holy Spirit to stem the tide in time, to nip them in the bud. The church will ever be assailed by the temptation to institutionalize its temporal prestige. This is a fact we should be aware of in advance, so that when the temptation comes we may be prompt to resist it. And we ought not to be scandalized (especially in a pharisaical way) if, here and there, and from time to time, men and women of the church seem to succumb to it.

Third, Jesus' temptation teaches us that the temptations of the evangelizer will generally be subtle rather than crass. More specifically, they will tend to present themselves as a good, a possible value for evangelization itself. A black-or-white choice between pure good and pure evil will be too obvious for a Christian. The most difficult temptation, then, will be that of a choice between two real and authentic goods, one of which will be incompatible with the lines God has traced for us, whether in the form of the criteria of his kingdom (recall Luke) or of our own personal call (Matthew's perspective). Thus, for example, matrimony is a positive value, as indeed is intimacy with a member of the opposite sex. But in the disciple whom Jesus has called to the commitment of celibacy, matrimony is a temptation. It is a temptation not because it is an evil, but because it is incompatible with what God wishes for this particular person. Similarly political militancy is good. But for priests and sisters it is temptation. Its method of promoting justice is not consonant with that of the kingdom. Where mission is concerned, temptations usually present themselves in terms of something that would be a good in itself, but is incompatible with the specific manner of Christian evangelization inculcated by the Beatitudes.

The second of the radical, basic causes of the interior suffering of Jesus is the *loneliness* that comes from the incomprehension and misunderstanding of others. We are not referring here to what might be called the "metaphysical solitude" of Christ—the Son of God himself who must hold converse with simple human beings. Nor are we referring to the simple "aloneness" that was of course inescapable in the hypothesis of so total and utter a dedication to mission. No, we are indeed speaking of the solitude, the loneliness, of a human being, but of a human solitude and loneliness that went incalculably beyond the incomprehension and loneliness that is the burden of the human condition as such. Jesus' loneliness became progressively more acute, all during the course of his missionary activity, in proportion to the misunderstanding, rejection, persecution, and abandonment to which he fell ever more and more victim in that activity.

The cross of loneliness Jesus must bear had two principal causes: his conflict with the religious/political "establishment"; and his "pastoral conflict," the conflict generated by the incomprehension of his own disciples.

Jesus' conflict with the religious authorities erupted in the first moments of his preaching activity. From the very start his relationship with them was polemical and hostile. Then it rapidly became a matter of open persecution. Finally, thanks to the collaboration of the political authorities, it resulted in his martyrdom.

It is the religious conflict that is basic here. The political one is secondary. That is, the latter is merely a function of the religious conflict. The religious authorities rejected Jesus right from the start. They deliberately distorted his words and his message. They "marginalized" him, excluded him from official religion. Thus Jesus was isolated by the primary addressees of the Good News, the very heirs of the faith of the chosen people of Israel. Jesus' love was frustrated in a painful trial of isolation and rejection. For "his own people did not accept him" (Jn. 1:11).

Indeed, "his own people" not only "did not accept him," they ended by persecuting him, calumniating him with the masses, denouncing him to the civil authorities, and finally doing away with him altogether. The cross is the ultimate symbol of Jesus' solitude among "his own people"—the ones to whom the messianic promises, which he had come to fulfill, had been principally addressed.

The root of this conflict, the root of the religious ostracism to which Jesus had to submit, lay in the fact that the God he proclaimed—his Father, the one, true God—was inconsistent with the distorted "God" of decadent official religion. The God of Jesus—a God of universal love and liberation, a God of the poor, a God of mercy, a God of the justice of the kingdom of the Beatitudes—was unacceptable to a religious establishment whose "God" was legalistic, ritualistic, formalistic, and manipulated by sectarian and political (nationalistic) interests. Every controversy Jesus had with these religious leaders, whether it concerned the Sabbath, rite and ritual, purification, the application of the law of Moses, gentiles and sinners, or what you will, derives from an irreducible incompatibility of concept of God and his kingdom. It is not by accident that Jesus is arraigned before the religious tribunal of the Sanhedrin as a blasphemer—someone who distorts the notion of God, and in this case someone who actually made himself God (Mt. 26:63–66).

If Jesus hoped for any understanding of his mission on the part of the civil authorities he was quickly disappointed. In Herod and the other Jewish leaders he aroused mistrust, or perhaps at best curiosity. The Roman authorities belittled him (but took care to keep him under surveillance). In the last stages of his mission, the hostility erupted into open persecution. Jesus had shown himself to have been a long-term threat to the interests of the dominators.

Jesus' political isolation and conflict are paradoxical, in view of his steadfast resistance to the temptation of a political messianism and his particular care to emphasize that his was not a mission after the manner of the mighty of this world. His kingdom, he insisted, does not "come with power." But his message concerning the absolute God relativized all earthly power, and his message on the dignity of all human beings, especially the poor, created a new sense of justice and a community of brothers and sisters, which was incompatible with the prevailing ideological views of power and the relationships of social groups. Jesus' message on the justice of the kingdom was a time bomb in a social world built on the abuse of power, wealth, and discrimination. Jesus stood alone before Roman and Jewish authority responsible to no one, and now so strangely allied against him.

But he is also isolated and misunderstood by all the Jewish political parties seeking liberation from foreign domination at the hands of the Romans. The reason was that he refused to be identified with them. The liberation he was promoting was so much more decisive, so much more radical. In the case of the Zealots, he rejected their terrorist methods. Before all these parties, too, Jesus had to suffer the solitude and loneliness of the prophet.

In view of all this, it is ironic that Jesus was finally sentenced to death by a civil court. But the indictments brought against him were indeed civil in nature. He was a political agitator, the allegation ran, and he had incited the people to nonpayment of taxes to Caesar. His sentence would be the one reserved for subversives (cf. Lk. 23:2).

But a proper estimate of Christ's loneliness and isolation can be formed especially from what occurred in his evangelizing activity itself, and in the teaching and training of his disciples. Jesus' most profound loneliness is a "pastoral loneliness." In his final days it will become painfully tragic. It arises from a misunderstanding of his message and from the failure of his disciples really to follow him. Even in the midst of the enthusiasm of the people and the admiration of the apostles, Jesus must suffer the interior conflict of being altogether alone. And in his hour of trial this was the greatest pain of all.

The first phase of Jesus' mission was the most "popular" one, the most gratifying one. He traversed Galilee from end to end, teaching the people. Here his mission began to take on the nature of an appeal to the masses. He adapted his preaching to the messianic expectations of the people. Its principal thrust concerns the kingdom of God, a kingdom of grace and reconciliation that would favor the poor and the afflicted (Lk. 4:18).

This is the period of the great discourses to the crowds (Mt. 5:1ff.) and miracle upon miracle to the benefit of the poor and oppressed. Here was a sign raised in the midst of the people (Exod. 13:9; Josh. 4:6; Wisd. 16:6) that the kingdom had come at last. And the people were filled with enthusiasm. They accosted him unceasingly (Mk. 3:10), they came from everywhere to follow him, even if it meant several days without a meal (Mt. 14:21). In order to be able to pray, Jesus had to withdraw to solitary places, and even then he had to do most of his praying at night (Jn. 4:42; 6:15).

And yet, John tells us, Jesus was mistrustful of these people: "Jesus knew them all and did not trust himself to them; he never needed evidence about any man; he could tell what a man had in him" (Jn. 2:24–25). Jesus knew that, basically, the great majority of these people were following him for mixed motives. He knew that they had not grasped the real nature of his message or the newness of the kingdom he was preaching to them. He knew that they were still doggedly attached to their ideals of a material, temporal messianic mission, that they were looking for a wonder-worker who would heal them of all their miseries. Even in the midst of the multitudes—upon whom, despite everything, he poured forth his overflowing store of compassion and mercy—Jesus was alone and misunderstood. The liberating love of God that he revealed to them failed to interest them as much as their immediate concerns.

The situation came to a head when, at the peak of his popularity—when he had multiplied the loaves—the people wanted to make him king (Jn. 6:15). Now Jesus fled. He resisted the temptation. He decided to confront the people with the truth all at once. He decided to present them with the authentic demands of his discipleship.

The encounter occurred the next day, in the synagogue at Capernaum. And here Jesus' disappointment and loneliness would plummet, and the upshot would be his abandonment by most of his followers.

> You are not looking for me
> because you have seen the signs
> but because you had all the bread you wanted to eat
> > [Jn. 6:26].

It was as if he had said, "You follow me because I deliver you from your material servitude. And indeed my kingdom does offer such deliverance. But it offers a great deal more, and this may not be the principal motive for following me." And he continued speaking to them of the nourishment he had brought them, and now was offering them, in the form of true life and liberation, which he referred to as his very body. He told them of the importance of having faith in him. And finally, he told them of the primacy of the spirit and spiritual rebirth (Jn. 6:44–59).

Faced with the real nature of Jesus' kingdom and the deliverance it offered, the crowds were shocked and scandalized. They grumbled against him. Now Jesus' abandonment became more open and obvious. He was criticized and contradicted (Jn. 6:41, 52). Even a good many of his disciples now left him. The crisis went as far as the apostles themselves. This was the moment when Judas lost faith in him. Misunderstood, Jesus was now actually willing to be abandoned even by the apostles, although it would have meant starting all over again. "What about you, do you want to go away too?" he asked them. But Peter, speaking in the name of all, responded: "Lord, who shall we go to? You have the message of eternal life, and we believe . . ." (Jn. 6:67–69).

From this moment forward, Jesus substantially altered the direction of his missionary strategy. He retired with the Twelve to out-of-the-way places, for now, he saw, he must concentrate on the training of the apostles themselves. Besides, "the Jews were out to kill him" at this juncture (Jn. 7:1). So Jesus no longer walked with the crowds. He worked almost no miracles now, and his discourse to the apostles grew more demanding. He emphasized a discipleship of faith and explicitly introduced the subject of the cross. But it is clear that, while the apostles did "believe" in him and his mission, they understood little of either. The evangelists repeatedly recall that they were slow of understanding (Mt. 16:9; Mk. 4:13; 8:21; 9:32; Lk. 9:45; Jn. 12:16; 20:9). They were still concerned about the coming of a temporal kingdom—in which of course they would occupy the highest positions of authority and prestige (Mt. 20:21; Mk. 9:33–35; Acts 1:6). Jesus' concern for their progress is inexhaustible. He is endlessly patient with them. But he is alone among them, misunderstood, and totally absorbed in the ideal he has received from his Father.

The drama reaches its crisis and denouement in Jerusalem, in the passion and crucifixion. Jesus finds himself abandoned by his apostles and all his disciples. Peter, their leader, denies even knowing him. His death overwhelms all with doubt and skepticism. Only Mary, who has accompanied him all the way to the foot of the cross, remains firm in faith and in the certain hope of resurrection.

Jesus dies on the cross helpless and abandoned. He even experiences a mysterious estrangement from his Father in this moment. "My God, my God, why have you deserted me?" he cries (Mt. 27:46). This is something beyond our grasp. It may be that it is an expression of the loneliness and abandonment in which Jesus had done his work and of the utter sense of dereliction in which he died.

But now the incalculable suffering of Jesus' abandonment is transformed into resurrection. Now this dereliction becomes a cause of hope for all and fertile promise for the church. We are able to understand and accompany Jesus today because, in his lonely martyrdom, he won for us the Spirit who dwells in the church, the Spirit who, Jesus said, "will teach you everything and remind you of all I have said to you" (Jn. 14:26). The forsaken of the earth live in hope today because Jesus died forsaken. For, in that abandonment, the Father caught up in his embrace every abandoned and rejected person on the face of the earth.

Neither the church nor its evangelizers have ever known, or ever will know, the extremity of the suffering of Jesus in his loneliness and abandonment. But they know that—like temptation—misunderstanding and the various forms of loneliness and abandonment are inherent in evangelization. These are what incorporate them into the redemptive deed of Christ. Missionaries are never altogether understood, either by the people they seek to evangelize, or by their own "disciples," or even, at times, by those in the official church who by vocation ought to understand and support them. The particular abandonment to which missionaries are vulnerable seems to come upon them when they least expect it, and from most unexpected quarters.

Loneliness and abandonment, as the highest form of "interior persecution," teach us to follow Jesus in the most fruitful phase of his mission: the laying down of his life. Even as the Lord, who sowed the seeds of the kingdom first with the crowds and then among his disciples, could not make it take root until he had laid down his life for it, so we ourselves, whatever missionary strategy we may employ, shall never see the seed of the gospel mature and bear fruit until we first surrender our own lives in the cause of the kingdom, day after day, even in the face of incomprehension, failure, and loneliness.

Epilogue

"ALL GENERATIONS WILL CALL ME BLESSED"

Now as he was speaking, a woman in the crowd raised her voice and said, "Happy the womb that bore you and the breasts you sucked!" But he replied, "Still happier those who hear the word of God and keep it!" [Lk. 11:27–28].

We have come to the end of our long journey through the Beatitudes. In Luke's version we have gained a better understanding of how God acts in human history. We have begun to see that God guides that history in function of his kingdom and that evangelization should therefore be guiding it as well, suffusing it with its own content, criteria, and options. In Matthew, we have seen the attitudes—the spirituality—of Christ the Evangelizer and thereby have discerned the path we ought to take to follow him in our own evangelizing endeavor.

Doubtless Jesus' Sermon on the Mount of the Beatitudes is a source of great missionary hope for us. Because of that discourse, we can now evangelize, under the guidance of the church, as Jesus evangelized, and know that the mission we carry out in the spirit of these Beatitudes will infallibly build the kingdom of God, however wrapped in the night of faith that kingdom may often appear to our gaze.

But at the same time the Beatitudes leave us with a poignant sense of loss. We experience a sensation, perhaps even a temptation, of hopelessness. Who of Jesus' disciples has ever actually realized the ideal of these Beatitudes in his or her own life? Who has ever really and truly believed in them? To be sure, the church, the authentic legatee of the Beatitudes, preaches them to Christians. But Christians are human beings, and human beings rarely practice what they preach. Deep within our Christian being, we would wish to see the Beatitudes incarnated in even one member of the church, or in one of Jesus' disciples, who, while belonging to the human race like the rest of us, and walking in faith even as we, would nevertheless reveal, by his or her testimony, that the Beatitudes are not a mere utopia, that at the end of a long journey they can become the reality of our life. We need to be encouraged in our hope by the witness to the gospel of some missionary who really acted in the spirit of the Beatitudes. But we find none, not even in the church. Or so it would seem. Are we confronted here with some manner of "idealism" on the part of Christ himself? Is this something that cannot be applied to the ordinary, workaday Christian life, so often banal and pedestrian in its manner and undertakings? Is this something incompatible with the realism of an evangelization that must be carried on in the dark of faith, and amid great frustration?

The answer is No. The Beatitudes are not just a call and promise offered to Jesus' disciples, and then left unrealized by them all. The Beatitudes *have* actually been lived and realized by a creature of our own race and a "believer," just as we must believe.

That person is Mary. Mary, the mother of Jesus, is the incarnation of the Beatitudes in a human being. She actualized them fully in her life on earth and thereby demonstrated that they are compatible with the human condition and calling. But this Mary, the perfect example of the Beatitudes, is not only the mother of Jesus. She is the mother of the church and the faithful as well. The church itself, then, can also be the concrete example of this same achievement and can in turn offer us its example as a model for our lives. For Mary is the prototype of the church and its Christians. She incarnates what the church itself seeks to be, and asks its members to be.

In Mary is reflected the perfect image of the Beatitudes and the perfect following of Jesus. She expresses this herself in her song of praise and thanksgiving to the merciful God who has chosen her as the mother of the Savior and to this end filled her to overflowing with his Holy Spirit: "Yes, from this day forward all generations will call me blessed" (Lk. 1:48).

What is the source of this "blessedness" of Mary's, of which she sings? What brought her not only to perfect fidelity in the following of her Son, but to a special participation in his mission as well, as Mother of God and human beings alike?

Her high privilege is rooted and based in her absolute fidelity to the word of God at every moment of her life. Jesus himself points to Mary's faithfulness as the source of her beatitude and grace. One day a simple woman of the people, desirous of extolling both Jesus and his mother at once, began to shout the praises of Mary's motherhood in its simple, human dimension: "Happy the womb that bore you and the breasts you sucked!" Jesus does not contradict this inspired person. What she has to say is certainly a grace and a "beatitude." But he takes the opportunity to tell us *why* Mary is "happy"—and thereby reveals the source of all "happiness," all beatitude: "Still happier those who hear the word of God and keep it!" (Lk. 11:27-28). The reason why Mary is the perfectly happy one is that she is perfectly faithful to the word of God.

For Mary's steadfastness is accomplished in the dark of faith, in complete poverty of spirit and abandonment to the Father. Mary is the consummate exemplar of the "poor of Yahweh," paragon of the hope abiding in the heart of the "righteous remnant of Israel." We have the paradigm of Mary's fidelity and openness to God's word in the annunciation. And this fidelity and openness will culminate at the foot of the cross, where "a sword will pierce your own soul too" (Lk. 2:35), and Mary's identification with Jesus persecuted and martyred for the sake of the justice and right of the kingdom will be complete.

Between these two moments of the annunciation and the cross, Mary grows. More and more is she the "happy" one, the follower of Jesus. She walks in faith and hope, consistently resisting the temptation to know the details of what God has in store for her. She "did not understand" (Lk. 2:50), nor did she seek to understand beforehand the precise, concrete historical manner of her approaching spiritual martyrdom, the culmination of her beatitude and happiness. No, she "stored up all these things in her heart" (Lk. 2:51), just as she would do with all the words and deeds of her Son throughout his ministry. Now this great heart, progressively purified and strengthened, leads her to the zenith of the contemplation of God her savior (Lk. 1:47) and the experience of his kingdom—the raison d'être of her existence and mission as mother of Jesus. The Magnificat itself has expressed her contemplative vision of this kingdom of mercy and hope for all—"He has come to the help of Israel his servant, mindful of his mercy" (Lk. 1:54)—her vision of justice and a special "beatitude" for the poor and the humiliated that will ill suit the idols of power and riches:

> He has pulled down princes from their thrones and exalted the lowly.
> The hungry he has filled with good things, the rich sent empty away [Lk. 1:52-53].

Mary is the happy one of the Beatitudes, the perfect follower of Jesus, by virtue of her absolute, steadfast identification with the mission of her Son. For in the annunciation, Mary receives and accepts a mission—one that will be consummated at the foot of the cross. And between those two moments she accompanied her Son in the whole course of his mission of evangelization, seconding his criteria and his options, sharing his attitudes, and identifying with him in his persecutions, loneliness, and martyrdom. Thus Mary is the only one ever to have come, gradually to be sure, to a grasp of the mystery of Jesus, his kingdom, and his liberating work of redemption. Mary alone understood the meaning of the cross, and of faith, for the building of the kingdom. She is the only one ever to have really, firmly believed in his resurrection. She, as no one else, has appreciated the value of the Beatitudes as the only path for the following of Jesus and the propagation of his kingdom.

By her radical fidelity to Christ and his mission, Mary, the happy one of the Beatitudes, is the concrete, historical model for our own pursuit of, and surrender to, mission. She is the consummate prototype of the church and of the Christian. She goes before us on our way. She accompanies us as a sister who knows how to inspire our continuous imitation and our hope.

But the "beatitude" and mission of Mary is not only in her fidelity to the word in the story of her mortal life. After all, it was in the annunciation that she received the fullness of the Holy Spirit (Lk. 1:35). For here, conceiving God within her heart by her acceptance of his word, she became capable of conceiving him in her entrails as well.

Mary is the mother of God made flesh and delivered up for us on account of the kingdom. Hence she is also mother of the church and its mission. Her motherhood and fullness of grace raise her condition of beatitude to sublime heights, infusing it with a permanent, universal quality that is altogether unique. "All generations will call me blessed," Mary sang, and she lives today in the church not only as a sign of fidelity and model for imitation, but also as a sign of the maternal dimension of God's love, of the mercy of God toward all human beings as tenderness, protection, and solicitude.

For God bends over us with a mother's heart. And it is Mary of the Beatitudes who incarnates, for all generations, the motherly love of a God who is that close to his children.